LONDON

By Aubrey Menen
and the Editors of Time-Life Books

With photographs by Brian Seed

THE GREAT CITIES · TIME-LIFE BOOKS · AMSTERDAM

The Author: Aubrey Menen was born in London of Indian/Irish parentage. He attended University College, London, where H. G. Wells encouraged him to become a writer. He became a director of London's Experimental Theatre for which he wrote and produced several plays. For the last twenty years he has devoted his time entirely to writing. Among his best known books are, *Rome Revealed, The Prevalence of Witches* and *The Duke of Gallodoro.*

The Photographer: Brian Seed was born in London in 1929, and except for the war years when he was evacuated, has lived there ever since. He joined TIME-LIFE at the age of 16 as an office boy, and later became the photographer in Europe for *Sports Illustrated.* He has also worked extensively for the London *Sunday Times* and the *Illustrated London News.* For the past three years he has been involved in making audio-visual programmes for American schools.

EDITOR: Dale Brown
Picture Editor: Pamela Marke
Assistant Picture Editor: Anne Angus
Design Consultant: Louis Klein
Staff Writer: Deborah Thompson
Researchers: Vanessa Kramer,
Jackie Matthews, Jasmine Spencer
Designer: Graham Davis
Assistant Designer: Roy Williams
Design Assistant: Shirin Patel
Picture Assistants: Cathy Doxat-Pratt, Christine Hinze

The captions and text of the picture essays were written by the staff of TIME-LIFE Books.

Published by TIME-LIFE International (Nederland) B.V.
5 Ottho Heldringstraat, Amsterdam 18.

Cover: a London bus is reflected 25 times in the leaded panes of St. James's, Sir Christopher Wren's church in Piccadilly.

First end paper: in twos and threes an elegant London crowd disperses across the parade ground after the ceremony of Trooping the Colour, the annual Guards parade marking the Queen's official birthday.

Last end paper: seen from inside, the sign on the door of an Edwardian pub's saloon bar is reversed amid graceful arabesques.

THE WORLD'S WILD PLACES
HUMAN BEHAVIOUR
THE ART OF SEWING
THE OLD WEST
THE EMERGENCE OF MAN
LIFE LIBRARY OF PHOTOGRAPHY
TIME-LIFE LIBRARY OF ART
FOODS OF THE WORLD
GREAT AGES OF MAN
LIFE SCIENCE LIBRARY
LIFE NATURE LIBRARY

Contents

1 | **The Heart of the Matter** — 5
Picture essay: The River of Many Moods — 22

2 | **Phoenix from the Fire** — 35
Picture essay: The True Londoner — 46

3 | **"The Great Wen"** — 57
Picture essay: "London in the Quick" — 70

4 | **Pomp and Circumstance** — 79
Picture essay: The Life of a Cavalryman — 92

5 | **The West End** — 103
Picture essay: The Londoner and His Parks — 116

6 | **Clubland and a Revolution** — 127

7 | **The Cockney: A Farewell** — 137
Picture essay: Where the Street is a Stage — 146

8 | **The Capital City** — 157
Picture essay: Landmarks Aglow with Tradition — 168

9 | **The Pride of the Londoner** — 177
Picture essay: The Candid London — 188

Acknowledgements and Bibliography — 198

Index — 199

I
The Heart of the Matter

I know London very well. Part of my life was spent there. But I have also lived in other great cities: Rome, Paris, Naples, Bombay, New Delhi, and I grew familiar with New York. I have returned to London again and again, for long sojourns of six months and more. Each time I returned, I understood it better. The other cities that I knew had sharpened my understanding—by contrast, by comparison, by the way their citizens were so different from the Londoner.

The essence of the Londoner who spends his life there—unlike me— is that he takes London for granted. That is not so with Rome: its inhabitants are always conscious of the history that lies about them. It is not true of Paris: the Parisian thinks that living there makes him a highly special sort of Frenchman. The New Yorker is always asking the visitor what he thinks of New York. The Londoner rarely does that: he assumes the visitor will like the place or he wouldn't be there.

As for the Londoner's own reactions, they are as misty as his city is in autumn. He has no phrases about it; not for him are such descriptions as "The Eternal City", "The City of Light", "Wonderful Town", words that the Romans, the Parisians, and the New Yorkers (in a good mood) will use. For an embarrassing year or two the Londoner found that his city had acquired a dreadful label: "Swinging London". It was with relief that he discovered all that was meant was a part of Chelsea and an obscure street of shops called Carnaby Street. Then it didn't seem to matter so much.

One night I flew in from Rome. It was a clear summer's evening, and London was spread below me, picked out in lights. It was a striking sight and the pilot pointed it out to us. The passengers said: "Look! London!" I said to myself, 'Ah! There's Hyde Park. And that's Hampstead over there. And that must be Camden Town and—yes—there's Whitechapel.' I was looking at my London: the town whose streets I walked as a boy, the place I explored as a young man, the areas that attracted me in my middle age. To me it is not one city. It is an anthology of places, each very different, to my eyes. When I meet a stranger on my travels in the world and he says to me, "I live in Paris", or maybe Vienna or Chicago, it is enough. I know him. But if he says, "I live in London", I always ask, "Whereabouts?" Then he knows *me*. I have spoken like a Londoner.

If you ask a Londoner about London as a whole, he will be vague, very much in the way that a multi-millionaire will be vague if you ask him how much money he has. The trouble is that London is so very big. Transferred to the moon it would be a blotch easily discernible by ordinary binoculars.

Dwarfing the twin cupolas of Victorian government offices in Whitehall, the unmistakeable shape of Big Ben rises commandingly like a lighthouse in a spreading tide of new buildings. In this telescopic-lens view, taken from the Duke of York's column in Waterloo Place, the Thames lies out of sight just beyond Big Ben.

Starting from Charing Cross, which is London's geographical centre, a determined tourist wishing to put the whole city under his feet would have 18 miles to walk north, 18 to walk south, the same to walk east and west, and even then he would know little about the place, having missed all the places north-west, north-east, and so on, points of the compass of great significance to the Londoner. If, exhausted, he consults a computer; it will tell him that he has missed approximately 20 square miles of territory, and most of its 7,397,014 inhabitants.

The Londoner is vague, too, about when this gigantic city started, but with more reason, for the historians themselves are just as hazy. It was not there when the Romans conquered Britain in A.D.43. Most Londoners do know of Queen Boadicea. She is a London heroine, because she beat the Romans in battle. What most Londoners do not know is that she also made a general massacre of the inhabitants, Roman or not. There is a monument to her near Parliament, the only monument in the world, so far as I know, erected by a grateful citizenry to someone who cut their throats wholesale.

That massacre took place in A.D. 60. From then on London grew until 18 centuries later, it was acknowledged as the leading city of the civilized world. It was until recent years, the capital of one third of the globe.

That time has passed. It did not last long: a mere hundred years or so, a summer season in the much longer history of Rome. Virtually all that remains of that hegemony is the Imperial State Crown, a jeweller's confection that weighs two and a half pounds and, as King George V remarked, is very difficult to balance on the head. Worn too long, it produces a pain in the neck, and that might have happened to Londoners had their city still been paramount. They have been spared that fate. The Londoner is not stiff-necked. But he is quietly aware that, in the words of St. Paul, he is the citizen of no mean city.

This is the London I shall describe. I shall journey through space and time. If you follow me to the end, I cannot promise you that you will know London. As another essayist has remarked, nobody can be said to do that. But, with the American Oliver Wendell Holmes, I shall hope that you will be able to claim that you know something of it.

On that night when I flew over London, there was one place darker than all the rest. The street lights shone but little else. It was as though some eccentric engineer had thrown a network of roads across a desert. I stared down at it, trying not to listen to the unctuous voice of "your captain" covering up for the plain fact that we were stacked up and waiting for a landing. He did not mention that this dark patch was the very heart of London, without which the vast twinkling sprawl over which we circled would never have been. This was "the City". My mind's eye needed no permission to land, to see it close-to. I saw its empty streets. I saw the caretaker making his way home from the public house, the policeman shaking door-handles and flashing lights through windows. I saw the cats. I heard the

This miniature, perhaps the earliest detailed view of the city, shows old London Bridge (background) and the skyline as it looked in about 1500. It is from a manuscript book of poems by the Duke of Orleans, who was captured by the British and held in the Tower of London beside the river Thames, where he is seen writing (right) and later leaving (left), after his ransom of 300,000 crowns had been paid.

silence. And I saw it as it would be in the morning light: the people walking to work—no, *trotting*—at that peculiar City pace; the traffic shouldering through its narrow lanes. I heard the dull rumble that is the special noise of London. I was a boy again, going to see my father. It is there that I would like us to begin our journey together.

It is a good place in which to start. London is big: the City is small. It is known as the Square Mile. It is not square, but a half-round, bounded by the Thames. It lies within the Roman walls that Boadicea stormed, and once comprised all London. For all that, it is not much concerned with history. Its business is that very contemporary thing—business.

Once, when I was a very small boy at my preparatory school, my companions demanded to know what my father did for a living. I went home and asked my mother. You must say, she told me, that your father is "Something in the City". This seemed to me unsatisfactory. It was so very vague. I was afraid the other boys would dub me the son of a Beefeater, one of those men in scarlet and gold whose picture was in our history books, and who guarded the Crown Jewels in the Tower of London. Interesting, indeed, but no match for the boy whose father was a professional cricketer and who had (or so he said) actually played at Lord's, that stretch of turf that is the Elysian Fields for every small English boy. Nevertheless, when the question was asked me again the next day, I said that my father was Something in the City, not trusting my voice very much. It was a success; rather too much of one. My questioner, who was bigger than I, said, "Oh, he is, is he? Then you can lend me a tanner, because I'm broke." A tanner was a sixpenny piece, and that, in those far-off days, about halved my weekly pocket money. But the son of Something in the City duly paid up. Later, when my father was preparing for one of his trips to the Far East, I peeped into his passport, and there read that he was "a City Merchant".

I filled out this picture for myself. We had had to learn a poem by John Masefield about a "quinquereme of Nineveh from distant Ophir". My father's office in the City, which I had never visited, was filled in my imagination with samples of ivory, an ape or two, and peacocks, and smelled of sandalwood and sweet white wine. It was very romantic and inflating and I lent several more tanners.

Some years passed before I was to see the City in reality. I was summoned to my father's office. It was a visit that was to be repeated throughout his lifetime, for it was his peculiar ruling that whenever we should speak of affairs between father and son, it should be done in the City, away from the feminine influence of home. His office was on the third floor. But it did smell of sandalwood, for, by a lucky coincidence, the oil of that wood was one of the things my father actually did import from far-off places.

His office smelled of sandalwood, that is, when the windows were shut. When they were open, it smelled of fish. Extending to the right of the street

Although Londoners refer to the familiar clockface (top) as Big Ben, the name properly belongs only to the great bronze hour-bell. The clock's 13-foot pendulum is adjusted to keep perfect time by adding and removing coins from two piles of pennies (bottom) that are balanced on the pendulum weight.

below was the fish-market of Billingsgate. Porters went to and fro carrying piles of baskets expertly upon their heads. Walking through it, I would stop my nose, but keep my ears open. For centuries, the porters of Billingsgate had been famous for their lurid and original swearing. I would return to school from these visits with a selection of red-hot oaths. I quite eclipsed the boy who had a Bible with all the dirty passages underlined.

Exactly opposite my father's office window rose a tall column on a square base. The column reached well above the building in which my father worked. I asked him what it was about. "That," he said, "is The Monument." "A monument to what, father?" "*The* Monument", he said severely. "It is the only monument in the world which is called, quite simply, *The* Monument. It marks the place where the Great Fire of London started. Well, not quite. If you pushed it over, that gold ball at the top would fall on the shop which started the blaze. The elegant figure you see carved on the base is Charles the Second. What do you know about Charles the Second?"

"Er . . . ." I said.

"Think", said my father.

"Er", I said. "Oranges. I mean, Nell Gwyn, who sold oranges and—er—became his mistress.

"I wonder", said my father, "that your headmaster has the nerve to demand the enormous fees I pay for you. Charles the Second, besides having the taste for—ah—oranges as you mention, showed quite remarkable abilities as an organizer when the Fire broke out. In fact, he stopped it by blowing up buildings in its path. He was careful never to show those abilities again. The City of London never liked its monarchs to be too clever. They chased his brother off the throne."

Then he took me to a place where he and other City merchants drank their morning coffee. I was proud to see my father hob-nobbing with the sort of men who had once assessed kings and fired them when they got too big for their breeches. In fact, I had a swollen head. When, in due course, my history master casually mentioned The Monument and said it marked the place where the Great Fire began, I put up my hand, rose, and said, "Not *quite*, sir," for which he never forgave me.

I went back there yesterday, 40 years on, as we sang at school. I paid my respects to the elegant Charles; I wandered through Billingsgate, reflecting that small boys were now encouraged to swear to relieve their complexes, then took another walk that I know. I went up King William Street, up Threadneedle Street where those City Merchants had for centuries banked their money, and then—should you wish to do the same, take a map, for it is easy to miss—I turned into a narrow alley that led to a small, quiet square with the magnificent name of Great St. Helen's. Great St. Helen's: not Great St. Helen's Square, or Great St. Helen's Close but just Great St. Helen's ("*The* Monument"; I could hear my father's voice in the silence).

At the far end of Great St. Helen's—and it is not so very far—stands

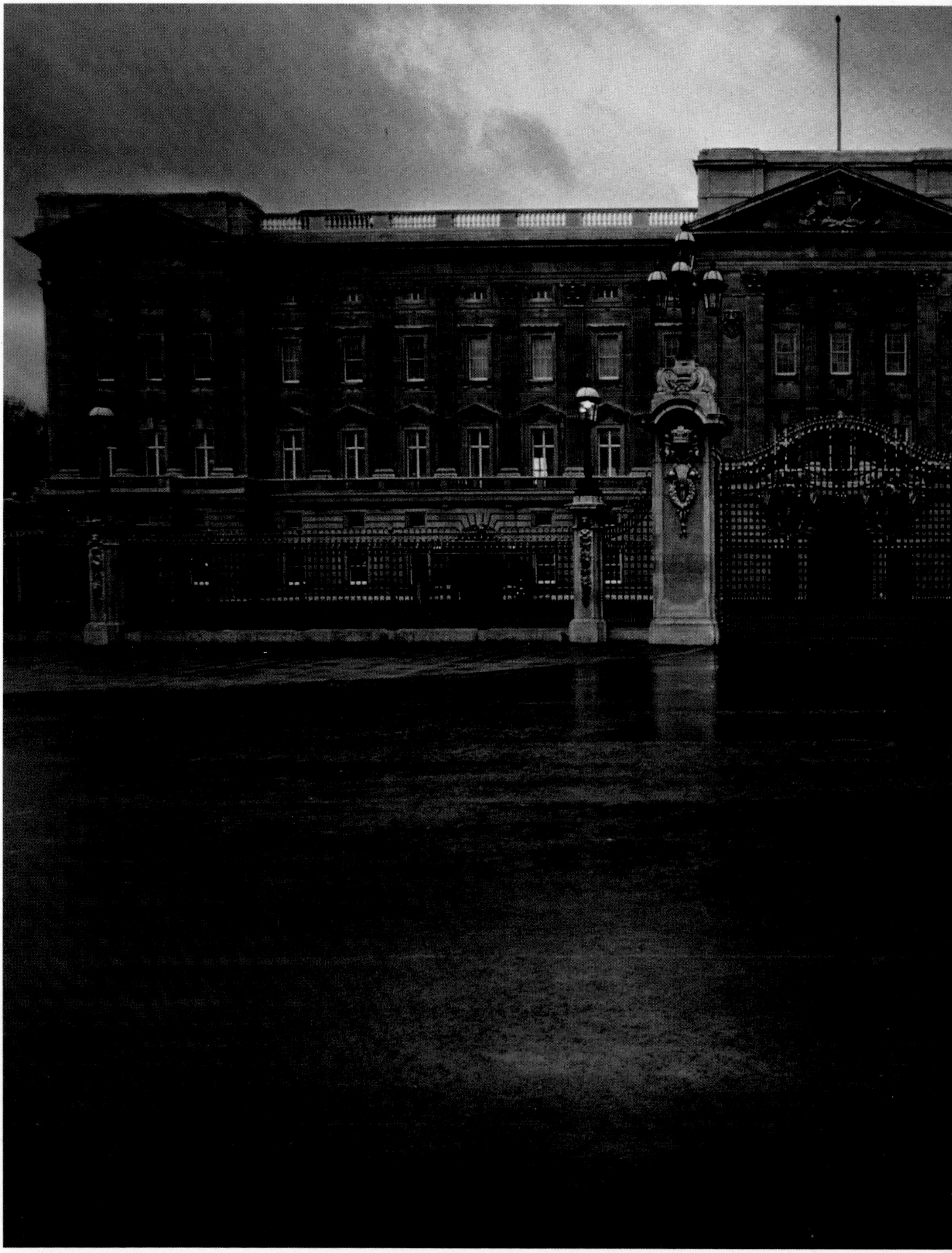

Buckingham Palace, London home of the sovereign since the accession of Queen Victoria in 1837, undergoes a change when the Royal Family is away. On a darkening winter's day, behind locked gates and rainswept tarmac, the familiar long façade presents a considerably altered appearance from the summer sightseer's usual view (inset), as shirt-sleeved crowds gather to watch the Changing of the Guard.

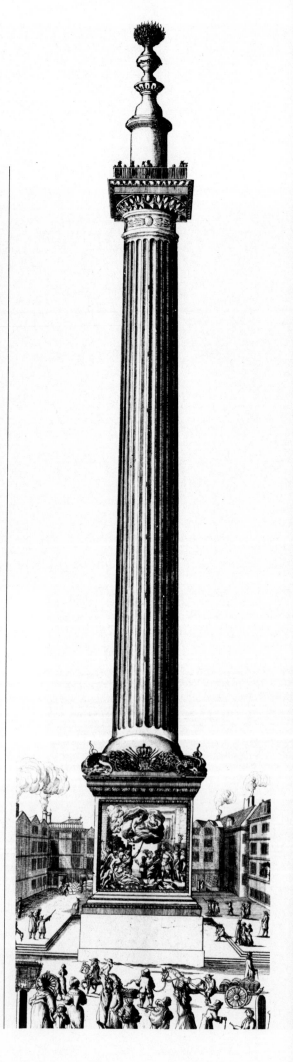

the church after which the square is named. It dates from the 12th Century: a row of battlements along the top give the air of a toy fortress. It must always have looked toy-like, but never more so than today, because behind it now rises a huge office-building of steel and glass—very cold steel and icy glass—that makes the brown stone of the church look warm and inviting. The foreign visitor who sees this unmerciful contrast might be scandalized. He would be wrong: the Londoners who built this church, and paid for it and are buried there, would have been delighted. They might have seen that enormous pile of offices in some happy dream.

Inside the church there are tombs, so many that St. Helen's has been called the Westminster Abbey of the City. Their effigies are there, brightly coloured. They are not all flat on their backs, like the kings and queens in that other Abbey. They kneel in prayer, heads up, man to man with God. With them are their wives and children. They introduce themselves and their families with proud, not to say smug, inscriptions. Here is Sir Andrew Judd. "Knight" is added in case you should miss the "Sir". He dealt in furs, and he went far in search of business. He tells us he travelled to Muscovy, prospered, became Lord Mayor of London. He was a man who, when he made an effort, expected it to pay dividends, even when it was made in bed. He had three wives. One gave him four sons and a daughter, the next "none", the third (a good businessman rebounds from failure) another daughter. These children dutifully produced grandchildren, and "in the month of September a thousand fyve hundred and fyefty eight" this worthy man died "worshippyng" (not God, let us note, but) "his posterytye". We can understand him. God was adequately worshipped by the nuns in the convent next door (there is the grille still visible through which they peered at the altar). He, as self-made man, worshipped what he had made.

Near him is Richard Staper. He is balding, he has a large nose, and a stout wife who gazes at him with an expression of great satisfaction. He was, says the stone below him, "the greatest merchant of his time, the chiefest actor in the discovery of the trades of Turkey and East India" (I drop the archaic spelling: business is business, and business depends upon communication. I shall let him get his message across). "He was humble in prosperity" (with that nose?), "painful and ever ready in public affairs, a discreetly liberal housekeeper bountiful to the poor, and an upright dealer in the world, and a devout aspirer after the world to come."

These were the merchant adventurers. Near by is the tomb of a business man who mostly stayed at home. He was Sir Thomas Gresham. He founded the Royal Exchange, and Queen Elizabeth I, well pleased, came to visit it. I have said that I went down Threadneedle Street. It runs by Gresham's Royal Exchange. Hanging over the pavement, high up, is an enormous gilded model of a grasshopper. It was Gresham's crest.

It was men like these who really built London. They made it rich. Monarchs might order palaces; but it was the City that lent them the money. Nobles might own broad acres, but it was the City that owned the mortgages, and still does. As William Kirwin, who was buried in St. Helen's in 1594, boasts from his tomb: "The fates have afforded this narrow house to me who have adorned London with noble buildings. By me royal palaces were built for others." It was through such men that London became the capital of the biggest empire that history has known. The Victorians said, "Trade follows the flag"—a nice piece of hypocrisy for, as everyone knew, the flag followed trade, to protect the factories, the trading ports, the bargains and treaties that the City had made. The Indian Empire began in a trading station in Surat, set up on the subcontinent's west coast by men like these who lie in St. Helen's. Some returned rich; some lie buried in Surat. Their tombs are still there, crumbling now, and instead of walking among them in the cool vault of a church, you must pull back the tropical grasses to read their epitaphs.

A few steps across Great St. Helen's and you are back in the present, and by that I mean very much in the present. At lunch-time the offices empty and the streets are crowded. I have mixed with the crowds, looking for the bowler hat, the striped trousers and the tightly-furled umbrella so beloved abroad as a symbol of the Englishman. They have gone. I found a top hat or two, but they belonged to doormen. The rare bowler was worn by the very young, jauntily, as if for a joke. The rest were dressed in the many modes current in London, the clerks with long hair reminiscent of courtiers of the elegant Charles.

I was interested enough to take one of these long-haired clerks to the brief lunch which is the lot of juniors in the City. Dress may seem a trivial matter elsewhere, but not in London. I knew that the bowler and the umbrella were not, in origin, a City uniform. In the early 1900's a guards-man (a soldier, that is, of the elite regiments in the British Army who guard the monarchy) had to salute a Guards officer when meeting him in the street, even if his superior was dressed as a civilian. The officers hit upon the umbrella as a secret symbol of their rank. The umbrella was rolled to excruciating tightness, and never unfolded, even in pouring rain. The bowler went with it, also a mark of rank, since it was derived from the panoply of fox-hunting. This curious rig was soon copied by the ambitious young with which the City has always swarmed—at which point it was dropped by the officers; nowadays they preserve it only for special occasions. I suppose a salute or two is missed but, in any case, the safety of the Queen is still assured.

Why had the city clerks, in their turn, dropped it? "Simple," said my clerk, as he gobbled. "I dressed that way for my first job. I felt very natty till my boss said, 'Leave the fancy dress to the sheikhs. They have the money; we haven't. If you dressed like that in Paris or Madrid or New York, they would think you were advertising British beer'. So, since I wanted to be sent to Paris and Madrid and New York, I dressed like anybody else."

What Londoners call simply The Monument commemorates the Great Fire of London. It was built in 1672-7 and is shown on the left in a contemporary engraving. In the densely peopled allegory on its base (below), Charles II in Roman dress directs the rebuilding of the city, personified as an exhausted woman (front left).

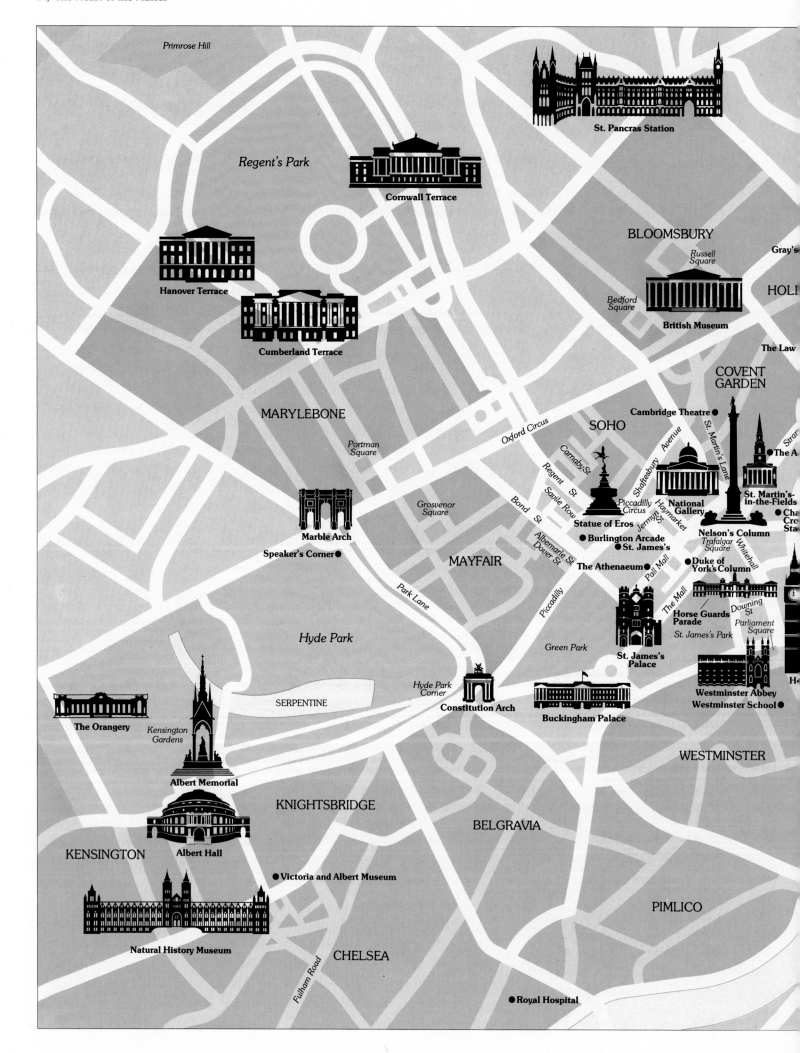

Primrose Hill

Regent's Park

Cornwall Terrace

St. Pancras Station

BLOOMSBURY

Russell Square

Gray's

HOL

Hanover Terrace

Bedford Square

British Museum

Cumberland Terrace

The Law

COVENT GARDEN

MARYLEBONE

Portman Square

Oxford Circus

SOHO

Cambridge Theatre ●

Shaftesbury Avenue

St. Martin's Lane

Strar

● The A

Carnaby St.

Regent St.

Marble Arch

Grosvenor Square

Bond St.

Saville Row

Piccadilly Circus

National Gallery

St. Martin's-in-the-Fields

Speaker's Corner ●

Statue of Eros

Jermyn St.

Cha Cro Sta

Nelson's Column

MAYFAIR

Albemarle St.

Dover St.

● **Burlington Arcade**

● **St. James's**

Trafalgar Square

● Duke of York's Column

The Athenaeum

Pall Mall

Park Lane

Whitehall

The Mall

Horse Guards Parade

Downing St.

Piccadilly

Hyde Park

Parliament Square

Hyde Park Corner

St. James's Palace

Green Park

St. James's Park

The Orangery

SERPENTINE

Constitution Arch

Buckingham Palace

Westminster Abbey

Kensington Gardens

Westminster School ●

Albert Memorial

KNIGHTSBRIDGE

BELGRAVIA

WESTMINSTER

KENSINGTON

Albert Hall

● **Victoria and Albert Museum**

PIMLICO

Natural History Museum

CHELSEA

Fulham Road

● **Royal Hospital**

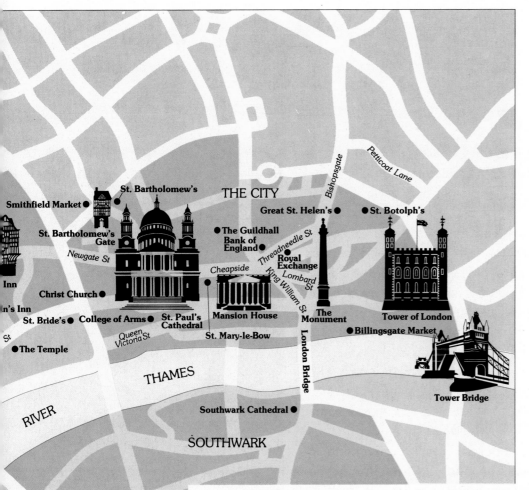

London's Green and Pleasant Town

The heart of London is shown at left, and the 610 square miles of Greater London are rendered in the topographical map below. Buildings, streets, squares and other landmarks mentioned in this book are identified on the maps. In the map at left, approximate boundaries of districts are also given.

The so-called City, the oldest part of London dating back to Roman times and now the business centre, occupies one square mile of territory along the River Thames. It was here that the Great Fire of 1666 began and destroyed nearly five-sixths of the city lying within the old walls. The map below includes all of Greater London's parks—some 40,000 acres of green oasis still preserved in the modern metropolis.

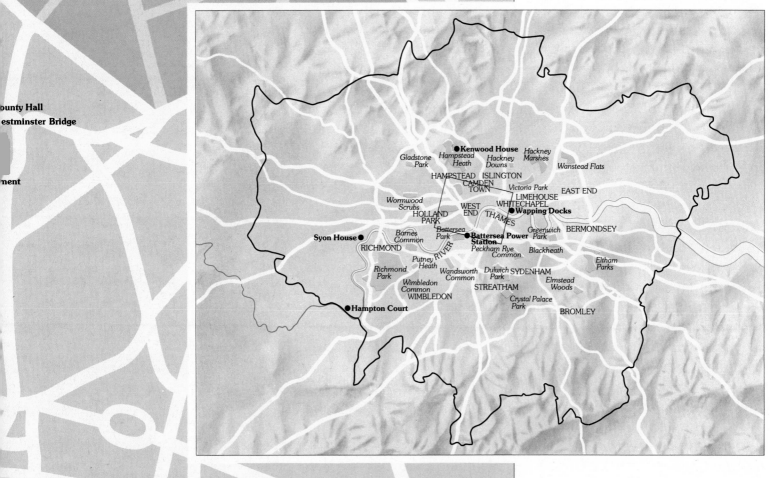

It is true that money no longer flows into the City without effort on the part of the merchants, as it did in the days of Victoria. Like their predecessors who lie in Great St. Helen's, they must go out and get it. But the dealers who sit at telephones in the glass boxes that rise around the churches are made of the same stuff as the adventurers. And the money they bring in, though diminished, is still important. The City, and the rest of London, is built on gravel, mud—and money. The Lord Mayor's state coach is bigger than the monarch's—and what is more, when he rides out in it once a year, he has a great big mace of silver-gilt sticking out of one window. It is as if the Queen of England were to wave the Imperial State Crown at the crowds as she rolled by, to show how much money she had.

But the City has never aimed at being genteel, or even aristocratic. The great merchants have bought themselves vast country properties; they have bought themselves titles, but at heart they remain merchants. Each year they elect one among them to be Lord Mayor, but they do not choose him for his ability alone. They choose a good, companionable fellow, with a solid wife who has a pair of sound feet to stand all the ceremonies and receptions; above all, they choose a man with a deep enough pocket to pay his expenses, which can be enormous. He is elected for one year—perhaps another if he can afford it—during which he hobnobs with the great of the land. He can be anybody, provided he is a city merchant and has the cash. There have been 640 Lord Mayors, and five have even been of foreign extraction. The City is broadminded. Dick Whittington's poverty is a legend, and his cat was invented a century and more after his death. But he was four times Mayor of London, and the legend reflects the fact: humble beginnings are no bar.

The relation of this monarch of the City to the monarch of the realm is curious, and tells much. From the time of William the Conqueror the sovereign had a palace in the City, but safely within the walls of the Tower of London. Later sovereigns preferred Westminster and Whitehall, which were outside the City; and in the Middle Ages, when the Lord Mayor was elected, he dutifully went in procession to the king to pay his loyal respects. The City grew richer and richer: by the 15th Century, the Lord Mayor no longer went to Westminster. His procession stopped at the limits of his own bailiwick. Later the City went even further in proclaiming its independence. When the monarch wished to enter it, he stopped at a gate called Temple Bar. There the Lord Mayor met him. He gave the monarch permission to enter what was after all his own capital, by handing him the City's sword of state. This ceremony is still carried out. It is well worth watching. The Lord Mayor in his robes and chain, and his entourage in medieval costume, outshines the Royal party, which can dress up no further than Service uniforms. It provokes the thought that the office of Lord Mayor is a far more stable one than that of the Crown. And of course it is a fact that no Lord Mayor has had his head cut off.

Lombard Street, the banking centre of London since Italian money-lenders from Lombardy gave the street its name in the 13th Century, is still lined with banks. Although the present buildings are 19th-Century or later, a hint of the medieval past lingers in the pictorial signboards hanging out over the pavement. These heraldic symbols once identified different business houses for customers before literacy was general. The spread eagle (bottom), for example, is now the international symbol of Barclays and here marks its home office.

Who are his electors? They are romantically named The Livery Companies of the City of London. The word "Company" here does not mean the incorporated sort but its members are, underneath the glamour and history, plain businessmen. Men of business all over the world have an inclination to club together for the sake of self-help, gossip and conviviality. The Companies of the City go under the titles of Mercers, Grocers, Drapers, Fishmongers, Goldsmiths, Haberdashers, Vintners and many more (including the Company of Upholders, or Fripperers, who were originally that useful body of men, the repairers of old clothes). These, clearly, were originally guilds, concerned with keeping their trades in good and honest order. But just as Elks do not clash their antlers in spring, or Rotarians pirouette like whirling dervishes, so nowadays the Companies do not have to function as guilds. Only the Goldsmiths, the Fishmongers, the Vintners and the Gunsmiths still keep a watchful eye on their trades. The Companies are now charitable institutions—rich, influential in the City and almost unknown and unremarked outside it. The outsider can, with suitable introductions, see the panelled halls in which the Companies meet, and he will be shown the treasures that they have accumulated through the ages. These consist for the most part in utensils for eating. Admittedly they are of silver and gold plate, and for the knowledgeable in such things, well wrought. But there are no great masterpieces of painting hanging on the walls, nor immortal statuary in the corners such as the visitor will find in the guild halls of the Continent. Interest in the fine arts for themselves came very late to England. In fact, it may fairly be said to have begun with Charles I, the father of that elegant Charles II whose figure I saw on The Monument. In the City it did not begin at all until very recent times. Upon enquiry, I have discovered that nowadays a few City merchants do collect authenticated pictures. The City has never really thought that there could be anything better than money; but, such are the strange times we live in, art, apparently, is now competing with cash.

The Livery Companies were composed of religious men. Most maintain a church; but one should not expect the miraculous edifices that the merchants of Florence and Siena insisted upon, and paid for. It is impossible to imagine the City merchants taking out Duccio's latest picture in joyful procession, as the Sienese did. The Golden Calf, perhaps; certainly it has had no more devoted worshippers since Sinai than it has today in Threadneedle Street. The City churches, despite the wealth of their benefactors, are all small. But they are of interest to the student of architecture, if only to illustrate the ingenious way that the builders put up something creditable on what was obviously very little money. Even these were allowed to fall into disrepair: in my youth they were covered in good London grime, both inside and out. They are now quite clean, and such gilt as they had has been refurbished. But that again is because of the strange times we live in; tourists today are even better imports than the spices of the East Indies.

Yet it is proper that the chief treasure of the Companies should be in plate rather than in piety. The high point of the City year is a gargantuan feast. It is called the Lord Mayor's Banquet, at which the great of the land outside the City are invited to meet the great within it. Traditionally, it is a time of vast eating and drinking. It once began with an expensive and heavy dish, a soup made from turtles. A recent Lord Mayor removed this item from the menu, not because (as we might expect) the dish was repellent in a world one third of which is under-nourished, but because he said that it was cruel to turtles.

The keynote of the feast is traditionally sounded by the current Prime Minister. He is announced (like others) by the liveried toast-master. Since English toast-masters (particularly those from the City) pick up quite a bit on the side by travelling to foreign parts to perform, it may be of interest to note that the gavel and stentorian voice arose because the noise made by drinking and eating aldermen could be overcome by no gentler means.

The Prime Minister's speech, silence having been obtained, is listened to with great attention. In it, he tells the City what he wants it to do. The Prime Minister, a busy politician, is not expected to understand the mysteries of high finance, while the Chancellor of the Exchequer is only expected to pretend to understand them when he introduces the Budget. Both are advised by the permanent officials of the Treasury, and these listen to the City. They are wise to do so. If they suspect that some policy of the Government will start foreigners making a run on the pound sterling, it is no use their ringing-up British ambassadors to ask if it is so; they can find out more quickly from the City. As one ambassador complained to me, diplomats are nowadays no more than office-boys, and slow ones at that.

The City will know. They will tell the Treasury and the Treasury will tell the Prime Minister. Woe betide him if he does not listen. The most striking instance of this happened in recent history. In 1956 the then Prime Minister, Sir Anthony Eden, for reasons that seemed good and sufficient to him and to much of the country, launched a war to regain the Suez Canal. It had scarcely begun when the City let it be known that in a few days he would have no money to fight it: the pound would collapse. He stopped the war, and was turned out of office by his party. Thus, when a Prime Minister rises to address the Lord Mayor's banquet, he hopes that the City will put more behind him than the gold plate lavishly displayed on the sideboard.

Of course these City merchants vary. But I have known them all my life, and think it is possible to draw a composite portrait of them as they remain in my memory. They are a breed all on their own. The New York business-man is nervous and taut; he will grow more nervous and taut until he has got you highly strung along with him. Not so the City magnate; he cultivates the relaxed manner. Nerves, like his appointment diary, are the business of his secretary. The City businessman gives the air of being fixed. He has none of the restlessness of the Milanese, who bounces continually on his

Messengers sprint from the Stock Exchange on Budget Day to brokers' offices clustering around it, transmitting the market's minute-to-minute reactions to the Chancellor's Budget revelations. A marked feature of business life in the small, closely packed area of the City has always been a reliance on personal dealings carried out by word of mouth.

chair. Nevertheless, the City businessman is not monumental, like the German. Like the Arab or the Indian, he mixes a quantity of small talk with his business conversation. He gives the impression of having all the time in the world, a characteristic that has been known to infuriate his colleagues in the New World. Equally upsetting is his style of dress. The woollen cloth of his suits is of a fineness and a richness that not even foreign millionaires can seem to achieve. It is a constant reminder that the prosperity of the City was founded centuries ago on the fact that the English broadcloth was the best in the world. Seen behind a City desk, it still is. He changes his fashion but, with subtlety. If the young wear very broad knots in their ties, his knots will slowly swell; the size of his lapels will broaden or diminish in gradual stages, so that he never looks in the fashion, nor out of it.

His manner of speaking can also be a stumbling block to the stranger. The big executives in the outside world strive to be clear and impressive when they speak. Each great English public school cultivates its own idiosyncrasies—charming in a boy but disconcerting in a man. The City merchant emphasizes whichever one he has learned. If he is a self-made man, he will emphasize the one he has picked up from an erstwhile boss. If he has a stammer, or a lisp, you must endure it. He usually speaks in a mutter. If you indicate that you cannot quite follow him, he will repeat his sentence in a bellow as though you are stone deaf. He will then resume muttering, only more so, at which point there is nothing to do but resort to lip-reading. In England's continual crises, he is much in demand for television interviews (as well he might be, because he is usually at the centre of the crisis), and here his way of speaking pays off. It reduces the brashest interviewer to a strained and ear-cocking silence.

In any other place—like Kuwait or Buenos Aires or Tokyo or where you will—the offices of the City businessman's opposite number are designed to impress you with the fact that a lot of money has been spent on furnishing them, and not so very long ago. By contrast the City office of an old-established firm looks like grandfather's sanctum. When one lights the offered cigar one looks around for a smoking-cap. It is homely, but the owner does not live there. Practically nobody lives in the City. By day it has a population of half-a-million. By 6 p.m. the population is no more than five thousand—it has been counted. Nobody has counted the cats.

The owner lives outside London, within easy reach of his office in his Rolls-Royce. But you will rarely, if ever, see that symbol of success in the City. The City merchant prefers to walk—the whole City of course is only a square mile. If he is elderly, he might take a taxi. A famous Governor of the Bank of England always used the public bus. In the evening the City businessman drives to a luxurious home which, as the 20th Century winds on its weary way, grows more and more to resemble a house on Long Island, with every modern convenience and those impossibly smooth and green lawns that put Nature in her place. In the office of one stockbroker with whom I have had a long acquaintance, one gains admission by striking a highly-polished Victorian bell such as was used to summon servants. One then waits in the outer darkness, surrounded by wood panelling, until some underling glidingly appears. But in my friend's country home, in what is known derisively as the Stockbroker's Belt, I also wait, while I am surveyed by closed-circuit television.

So much for my own impressions of the men who are Something in the City today. I find equally interesting the impression created in their opposite numbers in other great cities. Considering the economic state of England in recent years, I have found a most striking thing. No matter what the nationality of these foreign colleagues and rivals may be, they have a great faith in the probity of the City of London. Annually, this faith saves the rest of Britain from bankruptcy.

I suppose that the two topics the average Englishman today finds intolerably boring are religion and the Balance of Payments. But just as it is impossible to silence bishops, so, from time to time, the Londoner must read those yearly statements of national woe. Buried away in the report is always some paragraph, in execrable prose, which conveys that things would have been worse if it had not been for something called "invisible exports". This brings us straight back to the City, the Lord Mayor, the Banquet and the London businessmen. Invisible exports are the commissions earned in financial transactions, principally banking and insurance. The world trusts the City with its money—I mean, to handle it, not sit on it. For that latter, the Swiss are preferred.

This trust began in a coffee house. The idea of insurance is said to have started with a sharp man who could do his sums. A certain lottery was popular among merchants and in it there was one blank ticket. For a small sum, the man insured the merchants against this disappointment. The idea spread to shipping. In the late 17th Century merchants would gather in a coffee house run by one Edward Lloyd; there, among the cups and spoons, they would put their names to a document that said they would make good any loss. From this grew the great insurance company, Lloyd's of London. From this, too, grew that faith in the City, so that all over the globe the phrase "A.1 at Lloyd's" would mean security.

Lloyd's had an impartial way with them. They insured cargoes, even if it were a cargo of slaves. They gave Nelson a silver dinner service in gratitude for keeping the seas safe for British ships. But they also insured a client against Nelson's arch-enemy, Napoleon, should he die or be captured. Lloyd's also insured an enemy ship that had been taken over by the British Navy in 1793. The ship was French, and was called *The Lutine*, and in due course, it sank. Years later, its bell was recovered. It hangs to this day in the Underwriting Room. It is rung twice when a ship is feared lost, once if she later arrives safe in port.

Lloyd's is now a modern office block. The uniformed attendants are still called "waiters", in remembrance of the coffee house days. It is a touch of sentiment, an unexpected emotion in an insurance agent. But this large building itself is grimly functional, like all those others that are fast rising above the City. One would expect the businessmen to deplore the skyscrapers because they are changing the character of the place. They are out of scale; they are eating up the picturesque and narrow lanes that have marked the City for centuries. I have heard no complaint from the City merchants, except about the enormous rents that are charged.

I agree with the merchants. The City is not a place where one goes to admire art. Buildings that have some pretence to beauty do not detain one long. The Mansion House (the Lord Mayor's headquarters) has a handsome face, but it is pushed in to save space. The Guildhall is about as modest and retiring a piece of Gothic as one could find. The narrow streets have charm, yet if some of them go it will be no great pity. The City has always been a market place; it should never be a souk.

Still, there is one warren of lanes that I hope will be saved. The principal street is called Cheapside, because it was there that the main market of London was held, and haggling was the rule. There is not much to see nowadays. Cheapside was utterly destroyed by fire. But in it stands the church of St. Mary-le-Bow. The "bow" refers to the arches on which it was built, but it is the bells that catch the imagination. The true Londoner, the Cockney, is one who was born within the sound of them. In the quiet of bygone ages, they rang out much farther. Dick Whittington turned towards them when he heard them—he and his posthumous cat—and Dick was sitting on a milestone on Highgate Hill, a good six miles away.

On either side of Cheapside run little lanes and roads, which follow immemorial courses. They have names redolent of that most pragmatical of places, the City. They record the people who carried on their humble tasks there, made money, died and are forgotten, with no monument save their nameplates: Honey Lane, Ironmonger Lane, Milk Street, Bread Street, Wood Street and lastly, Friday Street, a reminder that the City was once Catholic, and ate fish on that day—carried from Billingsgate whose smell pervaded my father's office when I opened the window.

And as a harried consumer in a consumer society, I find it pleasant to know that when Cheapside flourished as a market, there was a pillory there for cheats. Butchers who sold stinking meat were put in it, and their bad meat was burned under their noses; bakers who gave short weight were drawn on a hurdle down the street, their loaves tied round their necks.

John Milton was born in one of the narrow streets that run off Cheapside, Sir Thomas More in another. But they were scarcely typical of the City. I prefer to think of Mrs. Beeton, she of England's most famous cookery book. She saw the light, fittingly enough, in Milk Street. Some Lord Mayor, having digested his Guildhall banquet, should raise a statue to her.

River of Many Moods

Through water flickering in the winter sunlight, four swans drift past Westminster Bridge, where the traffic is muted in the pearly mist of late afternoon.

Like all great urban rivers the Thames has for centuries been a working waterway. But it has grown less busy in recent years, as large-scale shipping has concentrated downstream from the once overworked Port of London, and the river has regained a measure of serenity. One day it may also regain a little of the purity that enabled early Londoners to drink from it. Still it is a river of many moods, viewed in varying lights and weather.

It offers a dramatic setting for the bridges that span it and the docks, jetties, waterworks, warehouses, power stations, historic buildings and dwellings that line its banks. Coiling imperturbably through the pleasant suburbs into the heart of the busy city, the ancient Thames unites them all until they become an indispensable part of its composite character—an inimitable mixture of Wordsworthian tranquillity and Dickensian brooding.

To a boy and his dog at low tide, the river is one feature of their local world: their own stretch of streaky water and muddy shingle at the end of the street.

Public and Private Thames

The well known vistas of the Thames—Houses of Parliament, Tower Bridge—are like public possessions, much viewed and almost too familiar to be seen afresh. But as the river meanders through the length of London it puts in a multitude of fragmentary, informal appearances—between houses, beyond gardens, behind warehouses—each of them possessively cherished, by the people who live in the neighbourhood, as the real Thames.

Late sun glows almost due west over the financial district, printing the familiar postcard outline of Tower Bridge upside down on the river's brassy surface.

The incoming tide pulls at the heavy barges on their moorings in the Rotherhithe reach as it flows up the Thames, and temporarily reverses the river's current. Rising and falling twice a day like a slow breath drawn in and out, the tide covers and reveals stretches of shingly shore and slickly glistening mud.

Hip-deep in mud and protected by high waders, an angler dredges the shore for worms to be used as bait.

A Breath from the 19th Century

Downriver from the heart of London lie the docks with their intricately interconnecting channels that once brought water for commerce and transport far behind the river's natural banks. Dockland with its own nefarious underworld flourished hectically throughout the Victorian period. But it has changed its character in the 20th Century and some of the older areas have finally fallen into disuse, visited only by a few bait-collecting anglers.

Melancholy warehouses flank a Thames inlet resembling a scene from Dickens. The flood dwindles at low tide to a trickle, here stranding a neglected barge.

A fearsome monument to 20th-Century technology, the mass of Battersea Power Station takes on an epic grandeur as it looms against the smoke-streaked sunset. Controversial when it was built in 1932-4 by the architect Sir Giles Gilbert Scott, it is grudgingly admired for its awesome spectacle by many Londoners who cannot imagine the river bank without it.

In the blue morning light the river at Hampton Court has a bucolic air.

Upriver Idyll

Withdrawing westwards from the city, great families built magnificent houses along the Thames in the peace of what was then the country. An inexorable urbanizing tide pursued them, lapping and passing the houses one by one. But in their parks is still preserved an idealized version of that rural riverside world through which the Thames threads its path towards London.

Dusk creeps over Syon House, 14 miles from Tower Bridge. Above the grazing cows the stone lion of the dukes of Northumberland gazes towards London.

2

Phoenix from the Fire

Everyone knows that in 1666 most of the City of London was burned to the ground. But what not everyone knows is an extraordinary thing about the event—which in effect was a quite ordinary thing when you understand the Londoners. And that was the fact that when the Great Fire of London had done its worst, Londoners were quite happy about it. They surveyed the smoking ruins in a spirit which can only be described by that very London word, "perky". In spite of the utter destruction of more than a thousand years of history and its monuments, the Londoners thought it was not such a bad thing (to use another London phrase) after all.

This must be explained, or the Londoner will forever be a mystery. And let me begin with a contemporary example. There is a district in London called Bloomsbury. In the first few decades of this century, Bloomsbury was inhabited by a most cultivated set of people. Such names as Virginia Woolf, Lytton Strachey and Roger Fry are world-famous, and they stand for the utmost in aesthetic refinement. As a young man I went to University College, which is in the heart of Bloomsbury. I walked its beautiful 18th-Century squares. I met the Bloomsbury Set. Roger Fry showed me his collection of French Post-Impressionists and described how he was fighting the English Philistines to convince them that these Frenchmen were not crack-brained daubers. While all this was going on, a great part of Bloomsbury was being ruthlessly torn down by my own university in order to put up a huge modern building.

I cannot remember that this act of destruction caused any stir among us. If the topic was raised at all, it was only to argue whether the architect was going to put up a building in the contemporary taste. And we were all as contemporary as tomorrow's milk. The building was finished and, though vast, was not big enough. The destruction of Bloomsbury goes on.

Again, in Queen Victoria's time, a builder of glass houses—his name was Sir Joseph Paxton—erected in Hyde Park the biggest glass house anybody had ever seen. It was called the Crystal Palace. It was used for the Great Exhibition of 1851 and it was so much liked that when the exhibition was over it was re-erected on a hill in the suburbs. Down the years, it was increasingly admired, for it was indeed beautiful, looking like a cataract that had been suddenly stilled. Then, one night in 1936, it was destroyed by fire. Londoners, at first, were very sad. A European architect has pointed out that it was the first truly modern building. I remember flying over the ruins in a plane, because I was writing an essay on it. Londoners were sad for about the traditional nine days, and then forgot all about it. The Crystal

Against a blackening sky a modern crane frames St. Botolph's, Bishopsgate, built in 1727-9 on the site of an even more ancient church. Everywhere London presents such juxtapositions of old and new, typical of a city that from earliest times to the present has been continually engaged in the process of renewal.

Palace could have been re-erected at small cost. It would nowadays be attracting the world. It has never been, and will never be, rebuilt.

I do not mean that we Londoners are insensitive to the pleasures of architecture. We—most of us, that is—simply refuse to become obdurate on the subject when the architecture is in London. When we cross the English Channel, it is another matter. Should some Italian town council knock down one medieval tower, we protest vehemently. I was shocked and indignant when I found a brash new hotel built in Amalfi, a place in which I had lived for years. Impoverished as England seems today, funds were briskly raised to save Venice; and cutting remarks were made when the Italian Government—intent on saving the whole country rather than one town, from sinking beneath the waves—was slow to use the money.

In London it is different. The Crystal Palace has spawned glass skyscrapers all over the earth. There are many in London: there will be more. The old skyline of London, low but for the spires of its churches crowding round St. Paul's mighty dome, was once one of our delights. By the end of this century this prospect will certainly be gone. And yet, as Londoners, we do not mind. Some of us have our regrets at the change, but they are not deep enough for us to stop the skyscrapers. Queen Elizabeth II once remarked that she now detested Buckingham Palace, because of the highrise around it. Her complaint awoke no echo in Londoners.

The reason goes to the heart of the true Londoner's attitude towards the city. We do not want it to be a museum. Its liveliness and its bustle are what attract us. Time and time again I have spent all the daylight hours admiring the loveliness of Florence, and all the evening wondering what the devil to do with myself, because Florence is so very dull after dark. That is usually the fate of a town that depends too much on its history. We do not want this to happen to London. True Londoners have begun to dislike the summer: that is when the tourist groups pour in and pass through our city as though it were dead and lying in state. We prefer the winter, when our abominable climate keeps visitors at bay.

I think that the Great Fire shaped our attitude as it shaped our London. Before it did its work, London was a clutter of half-timbered houses, with narrow streets and insanitary rivers. Over it rose the Gothic pile of St. Paul's, steadily falling into ruin and used in part as a place for money-changers and petty merchants. Could we see this vanished London, we would no doubt find it quaint and appealing, provided we could stop our noses. Nell Gwyn's oranges were as much for smelling as for eating. Elizabethans carried pomanders, which were small pierced balls of metal that held fragrant herbs to keep away the smells. The tradition, if not the odour, remains. Fresh herbs are still scattered in the principal Law Courts on one day of the year; and judges in procession carry nosegays, the very name of which shows what they were for. Only two houses remain of this 300-year-old warren; one is the Staple Inn at Holborn, much patched up but still, to

Boadicea to the Blitz: A London Chronology

A.D. 43	Londinium, a trading post, set up on the north bank of the Thames by the Roman occupiers of Britannia
200	Romans build the City's walls and gates
410	Rome recalls all military personnel from Britannia to protect the capital of the empire
449-577	London invaded by Angles, Saxons and Jutes
597	St. Augustine, sent by the Pope from Rome and welcomed by Ethelbert, King of Kent, becomes the first Archbishop of Canterbury
797	First invasion by the Danes
887	Treaty of Wedmore: Alfred the Great and Danish King Guthrum make peace. England divided into two kingdoms, with London the boundary
1016	King Ethelbert dies. Danish Canute becomes King of England
1066	After the Battle of Hastings, William I is crowned in Westminster Abbey
1170	Thomas Becket murdered in Canterbury Cathedral
1176	London Bridge rebuilt in stone, dedicated to Thomas Becket
1189	Henry Fitzailwyn is made first Mayor of London
1245	Henry III begins rebuilding Westminster Abbey in Gothic style
1272	Henry III buried in Westminster Abbey, establishing it as a mausoleum for kings and as the coronation church
1332	Parliament divided into two houses: Lords and Commons
1348-9	The Black Death strikes London
1381	Wat Tyler leads peasant's revolt, mobs sack London
1483	Princes Edward and Richard, nephews of Richard III, are murdered in the Tower of London

1530 Henry VIII takes over Whitehall Palace from Wolsey, deserting the Palace of Westminster
1532 Henry VIII builds a new palace: St. James's
1535 Sir Thomas More beheaded at Tower Hill, for refusing to accept Henry VIII as head of the Church

1558 Elizabeth I crowned in Westminster Abbey

1599 Shakespeare's Globe Theatre is opened on the South Bank of the Thames, at Southwark
1605 Gunpowder Plot, a conspiracy to blow up Parliament during a visit by James I, is discovered. Guy Fawkes and conspirators are imprisoned in the Tower of London

1649 Charles I beheaded at Whitehall. Oliver Cromwell named Protector of the Republic
1660 Restoration of the Monarchy: Charles II crowned in Westminster Abbey
1665 The Great Plague sweeps the city
1666 The Great Fire of London burns for five days, two-thirds of London is destroyed, but only three lives are lost
75-1710 St. Paul's Cathedral and 50 London churches rebuilt by Sir Christopher Wren and his assistants

1694 The Bank of England is established

1750 London's City Walls and gates are demolished, and the city expands towards Westminster
1776 Parliament receives news of the American Declaration of Independence

1805 Killed at the Battle of Trafalgar, Lord Nelson is buried in St. Paul's Cathedral

1820 John Nash, the Prince Regent's architect, completes his plan for Regent Street
1831 Newly-built London Bridge (replacing the old one, demolished in 1832) is opened by William IV
1834 The Palace of Westminster, Parliament's Seat for 300 years, burns to the ground—all except the Great Hall
1837 Victoria makes Buckingham Palace the chief Royal residence

1851 The Great Exhibition of All Nations is held in the "Crystal Palace" in Hyde Park
1852 Rebuilt Palace of Westminster is opened by Victoria. The Duke of Wellington is buried in St. Paul's Cathedral

1897 Victoria's Diamond Jubilee

1914 England declares war on Germany, beginning of World War I
1915 First Zeppelin attack on London
1936 Abdication of Edward VIII
1939 England declares war on Germany, beginning of World War II
1940 Start of the Blitz. Londoners suffer 57 continuous nights of air raids

1953 Elizabeth II crowned in Westminster Abbey

some degree, authentic. Its upper storey beetles over the pavement, in the fashion of the time. When two such houses faced each other across a lane, the path below was perpetually gloomy. The second survivor is more cheerful. It is the gateway to St. Bartholomew's Church. Londoners had covered it up and forgotten it until a Zeppelin bomb during the First World War brought it back to the light.

Imagine thousands of these houses, with open gutters below and chimneys belching smoke above. Those who believe that there is nothing new under the sun will be happy to note that pollution was even then a vivid topic of conversation. John Evelyn records in his diary that he noticed how some antique sculptures collected by the Earl of Arundel were being severely damaged by the London atmosphere. He moved them to a safer place at his own expense, and he tells us with pride of the honours that were done him by the learned for this act. He tells us too, in sombre notes, of the Great Plague that struck the insanitary town in 1665. The carts that carried away the dead are well known to everybody, as are the masked men who conducted them. What is not so familiar is what Londoners held to be the cause of the pestilence. Some thought it was the London air. The Lord Mayor lit bonfires in the streets to purify it. Their glare at night added to the horror of the creaking carts and the cry of "Bring out your dead", but did nothing to stop the sickness. This fact clearly indicated to many people (including John Evelyn) the real cause: it was the sinfulness of the people. Opinions were divided about which sins God was punishing. Evelyn, in favour with the Court, believed that it was the heresies of the Puritans under the leadership of the dead Cromwell; the Puritans, in favour with nobody but themselves, thought it was plainly the profligacies of the Court of Charles II.

The fire started exactly 202 feet away from where that figure of Charles is to be found today on the base of The Monument. The weather had been singularly dry for a long time. The first flames were seen at 10 o'clock on the night of September 2nd. John Evelyn had dinner with his family, who then got into a coach and went off to see the fire from a vantage point alongside the River Thames near Southwark. An easterly wind soon whipped the flames into a vast conflagration such as nobody in London had ever seen before. It raced through the streets until it reached St. Paul's, which being, as always, under repair, was covered with scaffolding. With this acting as tinder, the ancient church was soon burning furiously, the heat of the fire being so great that it cracked the stones.

"The conflagration was so universal", John Evelyn writes, "and the people so astonished, that from the beginning (I know not by what desponding or fate), they hardly stirred to quench it, so there was nothing heard or seen but crying out and lamentation, and running about like distracted creatures, without at all attempting to save their goods, such a strange consternation there was upon them."

Evelyn himself remained calm, as befitted a man of scientific bent. He was one of the founders of the Royal Society, in whose various halls many great discoveries of the modern world were to be announced. He was also the first to notice the phenomenon of the fire storm, by which a great conflagration seems to feed itself.

"So", he goes on, " . . . it burned both in breadth and length, the churches, public halls, Exchange, hospitals, monuments and ornaments, leaping in a prodigious manner from house to house and street to street, at great distance from one another, for the heat had even ignited the air."

Some Londoners fled to the country; some boarded boats on the Thames; surrounded by possessions, they watched London destroyed.

"God grant", writes Evelyn, "mine eyes might never behold the like, who now saw above ten thousand houses, all in one flame, noise and crackling and thunder of the impetuous flames, the shrieking of women and children, the hurry of people, the fall of towers, houses and churches was like a hideous storm; and the air all about so hot and inflamed that at the last one was not able to approach it."

The next day, September 3rd, the fire was still burning. John Evelyn went to Court so see the King, who put him and others in charge of doing the only thing that could stop the disaster. They were to blow up the houses in the fire's path. But property is property. "Certain tenacious and avaricious men would not permit it," wrote Evelyn, "because their houses must have been of the first." The picture of these merchants, gesticulating in the holocaust, their faces redder than ever in the glow of the flames, abides with us down the years.

The king had to step in, which he did with vigour. The houses were duly blown up, Evelyn doing Trojan work with a team of sailors. They could not, however, keep the fire from St. Paul's. It had six acres of leaden roof. This melted, and the boiling metal poured into the vault, which crashed to the floor. Evelyn, who was a writer of books, notes that the fall of the cathedral overwhelmed the chapel of St. Faith's. This was filled with books that publishers had carried there for safety. They all went up in smoke. (Two hundred and seventy five years later the city was once more ablaze, this time from German air raids, and again the fire storms raged through the streets and again the books were right in the middle of things. Publishers, essentially men of a conservative temperament, had not moved far. Their books were now stored in Paternoster Row hard by the cathedral. The bombs fell, and once more there was a great burning of books.)

Evelyn made his way through the ruins, so hot that his hair was almost singed, out into the country where he saw "two hundred thousand people of all ranks and degrees, dispersed and laying along by their heaps of what they could save from the *Incendium*, deploring their loss, and though ready to perish from hunger and destitution, yet not asking one penny for relief". "This", mused Evelyn with considerable acumen, "appeared a stranger

A German bomber rains its load on to Thameside docks and railways. East End dockland residents suffered more than any other Londoners during the Blitz.

The library of Holland House is a mass of wreckage after a 1941 air raid on West London, yet intrepid bibliophiles continue to browse among the debris.

sight to me than any I had yet beheld." Stranger, that is, than the Great Fire itself, and he was correct. The Londoner is calm in a crisis, with a stoicism that was to puzzle Hitler when he started a new fire of his own.

Not that they were supine. There was a brief, scattered outburst of what a Londoner would call bad temper, at the time. Britain was at war with the French and the Dutch. Word went round that it was these, and not God, who had caused the fire. Some Londoners flocked back to the City and slaughtered a few Frenchmen and Dutch. These hotheads took a great deal of soothing, Evelyn doing his best. "I left them", he says, "pretty quiet, and came home to my house, sufficiently weary and broken."

We may well believe him. The astonishing thing is that four days later he presented himself to King Charles with a survey of the ruins and a plan for its rebuilding. The king was most interested, gave him dinner, and then sent him off to the queen's bedchamber. She listened to him for a whole hour and was extremely pleased. Then she went off for a ride "to take the air", which by now was presumably once more breathable. She was dressed as a Cavalier, in riding habit, hat, feather and horseman's coat.

I mention that last detail because it has a sequel. Such was the phlegm of the Court in face of the disaster that one month later, with the houses still smoking and the ruins of St. Paul's tottering to everyone's danger, King Charles presented himself to the amazed Evelyn dressed as a Persian. He had put himself ("solemnly" says Evelyn) into a waistcoat with a sash, garters and buckles set with gems. The reason he gave was that he had hitherto dressed in the French fashion, but since his kingdom was at war with France, this would no longer do. He advised his courtiers to do the same. God may have punished London—a week before the king had ordered a general day of fasting for its sins—but, being London, there was to be no sackcloth; ashes, of course, were there in plenty. Then all the Court went off to see a play. Evelyn was scandalized to find the female parts acted by women, not boys. (In the next great fire that Londoners were to suffer they were very proud of a theatre showing burlesque, which boasted that in spite of the bombardments, "We never closed").

In fact, this is the Londoner at his best and perhaps most mystifying: no matter how great the catastrophe, the Londoner takes it in his stride, and calmly sits restoring the *status quo*. Evelyn did not follow up his plan. It was for improving London. A rigid, geometrical affair, and perhaps it is as well that it was dropped. Evelyn himself found that he had more important fish to fry in his Royal Society. Early next year we find him absorbed in an experiment for lifting huge stones with gunpowder.

Still, London had to be rebuilt. It was an age of inspired amateurs and the rebuilding was put into the hands of the most inspired amateur of them all, Sir Christopher Wren. He is a Londoner's hero. To tell the truth, his is the only name among architects that the average Londoner can remember. Wren never trained as an architect. He was a frail little man, but with a

Legend long held that if ravens like these at the Tower of London should leave, the British Empire would collapse. The empire is gone but the ravens are still there—six of them, cared for by a Raven Master, their wings clipped to prevent flight. Their presence seems assured: when one dies, a replacement is brought in.

resilient constitution. Before the Fire he had run up a couple of buildings at Oxford, his university, without knowing very much about how it was done. They are moderately successful and, at any rate, they still stand. He had paid a visit to France. The French set the style for everything in Europe, and in architecture the French copied the Italians. So Wren studied prints of buildings in Rome, some of which gave a false impression of what these actually looked like, as we can see by comparing the 17th-Century pictures with the buildings today. But they were enough for this extraordinary man. From the Italians he took his notions for rebuilding St. Paul's, from the French his plan for rebuilding London.

This latter was a magnificent affair of great avenues centring on circular open spaces. The king approved but the plan was never carried out. St. Paul's, however, was finished in Wren's own long life-time. It is acknowledged to be one of the most beautiful buildings ever erected.

An architect is engaged in a very chancy business. What he puts up will stay up for a long time, and it is likely to be conspicuous. Whether future generations will consider him a genius or a public nuisance is a matter of luck. He must build according to the taste of the time because he builds with somebody else's money, and the man who pays the piper calls the tune, even if, to continue the metaphor, he has a tin ear. No patron wishes to be thought old-fashioned. So an architect is very much in the position of a designer of women's dresses, except that his lot is a little worse. Some women can be bullied into wearing anything, while a patron, laying out large sums of money, has the whip-hand. An architect spends a great deal of his life doing as he is told, and sometimes, as with St. Paul's he must be the servant of many masters.

The taste of Wren's time was for the logical and clear. Science, although young, was fashionable. Seven years after the Great Fire the Royal Society was to elect as a member one Isaac Newton who had recently proved that light was made up of seven colours, and who was to announce the law of gravitation (and who was to spend a great deal of the rest of his time trying to show that the future could be predicted from the Book of Daniel.)

To Wren's generation, the Gothic style was considered barbarous and not logical at all. What was the point of putting up cathedrals with bigger and bigger windows and then filling them with coloured glass so that inside you often could barely discern the face of your neighbour? The 17th Century wanted space and light. The style that Bramante and Michelangelo had evolved for the Popes was more to be preferred. Charles II asked Wren to rebuild St. Paul's, and there was no doubt among men of taste as to what it should look like. It must look like St. Peter's, Rome.

Now I have spent countless hours in St. Peter's. I have gone over it stone by stone. With the reluctant permission of cardinals I have explored that hidden world of corridors, staircases and rooms that have been made inside its massive walls and still more massive piers. I have spent hours with the man who looks after it and heard all his housekeeping problems. It is an awesome masterpiece. But I have never felt at home there.

Approaching St. Paul's up Ludgate Hill on which it stands, I have the same impression as its bulk looms nearer and nearer. I feel that I shall go inside and I shall be diminished. Yet when I do go inside I am not. It is very big; I can see that. But I do not feel as though I am Jonah in the belly of the whale, as I do in St. Peter's. I can measure myself against it, and feel at home. I can sit in St. Paul's and read a book that has nothing to do with religion. I do not believe anybody has done that in St. Peter's.

Wren lies buried in St. Paul's. His tomb is a plain slab of stone on which is written: "If you seek his monument, look around you." It is a pity the words are in Latin. They should be in English, for Wren was very much an Englishman. He took his designs from Rome but, with splendid insularity, he never went there. Perhaps that is why he built St. Paul's without the Latin rhetoric that goes so well with Rome's bold light but that would never have done for London.

Architecture, first and last and all the time, is proportion. Wren's pro-portions—in his columns, his mouldings, his decorations—all have delicacy. They are well-bred, well-mannered and discreet. His dome, when he built it, was the third largest in the world. Yet such was Wren's genius that he managed to give it an air of modesty. In the history of architecture, the style that Wren used is known as the Baroque, but it is a word that comes uneasily to one's lips when looking at St. Paul's. The Baroque style is an immense elaboration of the manner in which the classical Romans built. So is St. Paul's: here are the columns, the friezes, the carved swags, the curves and counter-curves of the Baroque. But it is as though a fugue that was written for a mighty organ is being played on a piano in some quiet drawing room. It is the perfect cathedral for London.

Wren had his troubles, He wanted to make the cathedral in the shape of a cross with equal arms, as Michelangelo had wanted for St. Peter's. The clergy protested. Everybody knew the proper shape for a cathedral: it was a cross with three short arms and one long one. Wren, being a mere architect, had to obey. It led him to commit an architect's cardinal sin, which is to build something that looks like something it is not. The upper storey, from the outside, looks as though it is solid with the church. It is merely a screen. The roofs of the aisles behind it are much lower. Wren, however, was right. If the cathedral had really been as big as it looks from the outside, it would have been much too big inside.

Wren's never-executed plan for the rebuilding of London called for wide streets, huge piazzas and long perspectives. If the burghers of London had been unwilling to have their homes blown up during the Fire, they were certainly not going to have them torn down when the fire was out. Even those who no longer had a house clung fiercely to their property. And this time the king found he had no powers to make them give it up.

Before today's skyscrapers, London's skyline was largely the creation of a single genius: Christopher Wren. Many of his church spires are compared with St. Paul's dome in this 19th-Century engraving. In spite of appearances in the engraving, the highest is St. Bride's (far right) at 226 feet, followed by St. Mary-le-Bow (next to the dome), just one foot shorter.

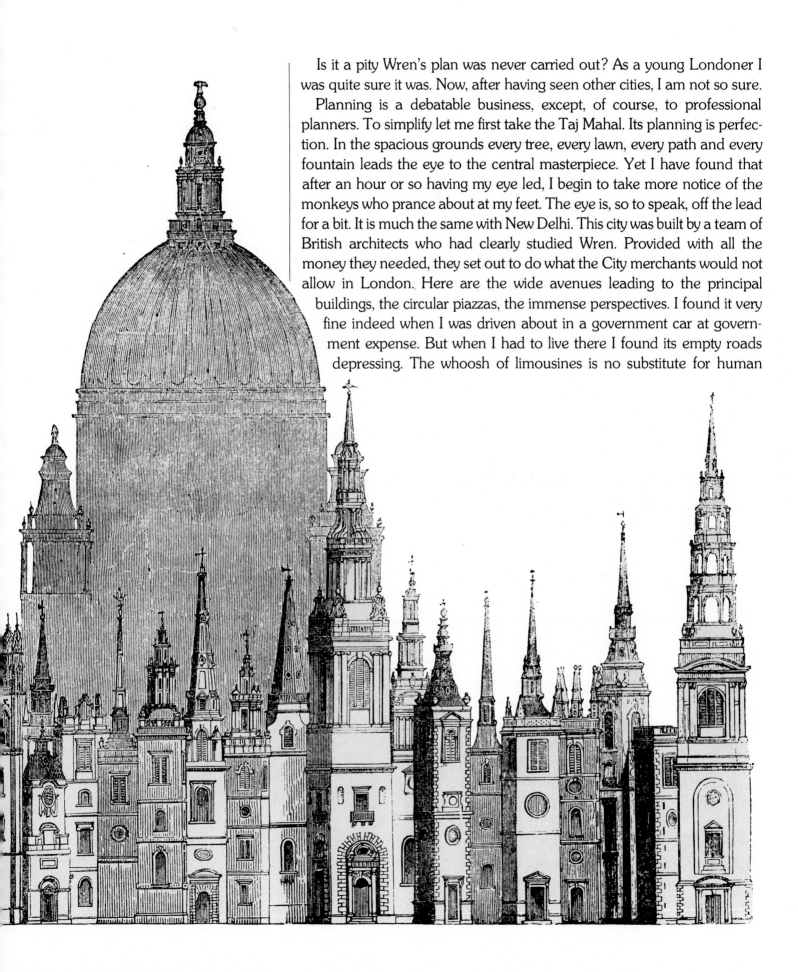

Is it a pity Wren's plan was never carried out? As a young Londoner I was quite sure it was. Now, after having seen other cities, I am not so sure.

Planning is a debatable business, except, of course, to professional planners. To simplify let me first take the Taj Mahal. Its planning is perfection. In the spacious grounds every tree, every lawn, every path and every fountain leads the eye to the central masterpiece. Yet I have found that after an hour or so having my eye led, I begin to take more notice of the monkeys who prance about at my feet. The eye is, so to speak, off the lead for a bit. It is much the same with New Delhi. This city was built by a team of British architects who had clearly studied Wren. Provided with all the money they needed, they set out to do what the City merchants would not allow in London. Here are the wide avenues leading to the principal buildings, the circular piazzas, the immense perspectives. I found it very fine indeed when I was driven about in a government car at government expense. But when I had to live there I found its empty roads depressing. The whoosh of limousines is no substitute for human voices or human footsteps. I moved to the tangled lanes of Old Delhi. There, admittedly, I was sometimes awakened by a street brawl, and once by a string of camels eating my flowering plants. Still, I liked it better.

Rome was, in part, laid out by the Popes, and in part by Mussolini, both having the same aim—to have fine settings for parades. Nearly all foreigners, settling in Rome, first take apartments in palaces bordering these arteries. After a year or two, they move to the winding lanes and tottering buildings of Trastevere, once a slum, or (as I did) to the old Jewish ghetto. Washington is spaciously designed; but my friends there, when they can afford it, live in Georgetown, a creditable replica of 18th-Century London. Brasilia is a triumph of modern planning, an entirely 20th-Century capital; motor cars enjoy it immensely, but people live there only when the government forces them to. I am told by one who has suffered this experience that the residents are making their own twisty lanes by walking through government buildings instead of by the boulevards. The mention of boulevards brings Paris to mind. Paris was planned, and I can find nothing to say against it. But then, it is filled with volatile Parisians. They invented the side-walk café, and subsequently the game of throwing the chairs and tables at one another for political reasons. Verve like that will enliven the best-planned town.

While Wren's London never came into being, he was fortunate in being able to finish St. Paul's. Taste was changing, and before he died, he was dismissed from his post. St. Paul's is not entirely as he wished it. The grumbling old man was forced to add those finicky balustrades which show up more in photographs than to the naked eye. Wren, speaking bitterly of them, said, "Ladies think nothing well without an edging."

The overriding fashion for Baroque was now over. Italian taste was still the fashion, but the Italians themselves had changed. Palladio, an architect of refined instincts, had invented a style based on classical Roman examples, resulting in houses which, although large, could with comfort be lived in—something not always possible in the great palaces of the Baroque. The Palladian style appealed to the English who, because of their climate, lived more inside their homes than the Italians did. Talented men such as Robert Adam and John Nash mastered the style and, in the matter of interior decoration, improved upon it. Nash was quite a planner. He built a sweeping road, Regent Street, which led in a fine perspective to a circular church and beyond that to another great circle of Palladian houses surrounding a park. London has got the better of him, as it has of all artists who have tried to dictate to her. Nash's Regent Street has given way to a double Chinese Wall of shops. The park—Regent's Park—remains, for although Londoners tore up the plans of architects, they have always clung fiercely to their open spaces. At school we learned a story, no doubt apocryphal, but nonetheless effective. A queen asked how much it would cost to resume proprietorship of Hyde Park and Kensington

Gardens, once in the Royal domain. "Two crowns, ma'am", she was told—meaning not ten shillings but the crowns of Scotland and England. So we still have Nash's Regent's Park and his houses around it.

Robert Adam has also been lucky. Kenwood House, perched up on Hampstead Heath, still shows to great advantage his exquisite taste. The interior might even be called feminine (but without "the edging"). I cannot recall any place that is so desirable to live in.

There was nothing feminine about Adam himself. He was a property developer, and a tough one. He and his brother, John, took a stretch of mud and clay on the banks of the Thames and turned it into terraced residences, called The Adelphi. It was a triumphantly successful essay in domestic architecture, perfectly adapted to its site by the flowing Thames. Most of it remains, the building now occupied by the Royal Society of Arts still being a fine example of Adam's gifts.

There were other property developers at work. They were not on Adam's level, but they were not far below it. Wren, Adam, Nash and the successors rebuilt London—from scratch. Shakespeare's London no longer exists and it is unrewarding to look for it. The Great Fire settled that matter, and Londoners showed no nostalgia for what it swept away. True, they put up The Monument, but it was something of an afterthought. Wren intended the column to be an enormous telescope, but the project failed, and the present column was the thrifty result. The place where the Great Fire stopped is marked by a little monument so unobtrusive that it perfectly expresses the fact that Londoners forgot the disaster as soon as they could. It is the statue of a naked infant, in which we can perhaps see a symbol of London's re-birth. But it is also symptomatic of the Londoner who calmly rebuilt after the fire that these citizens today, when they know of the statue's existence at all, call it merely "The Fat Boy".

The True Londoner

Under the ruby radiance of a sunshade, the genteel grimace of a lady leaving church manages to combine conventional civility with indomitable self-reliance.

Among the city's seven million infinitely varied inhabitants, who are the true Londoners? Any attempt to characterize them must rest on an intuitive generalization; even so, there is a widely shared belief that a London character, a London attitude, does exist. And the proof of it often lies in a gesture, a glance or a fleeting exchange. Here indeed are the people for whom resourcefulness, comradeship and humour are inborn traits, although it may take an emergency to bring them out, for they are often overlaid by conventional reserve. As these photographs suggest, the Londoner has the gaiety to dress for any occasion and the assertiveness to be himself in any guise. He can absorb a part of London's tradition and make it completely his own—and this quality is among the attributes that make the Londoner true to his city and to himself.

A night's sleep in the warm park, a sunny morning and sparkling wine for breakfast can put any London tramp in the best—and most expansive—of spirits.

A slight twinkle behind the deadpan expression of the jellied-eel seller betrays the humour hidden in the gruff remarks he dispenses with his vinegar and salt.

A living monument to himself, a Chelsea Pensioner displays quiet pride in his years of service as a soldier.

Parading in historic uniform, a veteran member of London's noble fire brigade reveals some of the melancholy, as well as the dignity that goes with being old.

Sunk in preoccupation, oblivious of his picturesque appearance and surroundings, a young barrister demonstrates the stiff upper lip essential to his career.

Already playing a role in society, a young man taking part in a London wedding projects a half-understanding realization of his elders' sense of responsibility.

Four Cockney porters express their infectious joie de vivre by a bit of horseplay in the Smithfield meat-market.

Between an off-duty Guards officer and the chaplain of his regiment, companionship is restrained, as they walk in the quiet dappled sunlight of the Mall.

3

"The Great Wen"

After the Fire, London rose again; and it grew. The architects who rebuilt it were far from getting their own way. But besides Wren's churches and his great cathedral, they left behind them one of present-day London's greatest pleasures, its "Georgian" squares.

Properly speaking, "Georgian" is not the right word. But it is a London word, and the Londoner is not pedantic. The places he so describes were built not only under Queen Anne and the Georges, but under William IV and even Victoria. To us, however, the sober, harmonious terraces, the well-placed windows, the porticos and the quiet gardens they surround are known as "Georgian". It is, most of all, an affectionate name.

Soon after the Great Fire, it was seen that London could no longer stay within its city walls. It had already spread along the sandy Thameside beach called the Strand and reached Westminster, where the monarch lived. Ruling the roost for the next century and beyond were the great nobles—the dukes, earls and marquises. They lived mostly in their country houses and greatly preferred them to London, which was becoming increasingly noisy and smoky, as the population grew. Still, the King was in London, and to London the nobles had to go, lest, like Queen Elizabeth I, the monarch come to them and eat them out of house and home.

So the nobles bought property and built town-houses for themselves, well outside the walls. They also built other houses for profit. Mayfair was a village; it was soon covered with houses. The houses were let to lesser aristocracy at satisfactory rents, or were leased. The leases usually ran for 99 years; after one year less than a century the house and land reverted to the original ownership. It would seem a bad bargain for the heirs of the lessee. But England in the 17th, 18th and 19th Centuries was full of euphoria; it enjoyed a prolonged boom. True, an economist can find periods of depression, but the slumps were never busts. On the whole, the upper classes grew richer and richer, and so did London. In 99 years it could reasonably be hoped that the lessee's heirs would be wealthy enough to buy their own lands and be property developers themselves.

The parts of London those big and little aristocrats built can still be seen. Many of them are charming. Thus, I know of no other city in the world where being mixed up in a lawsuit can soothe the spirit—not, of course, in the lawyers' offices, but just outside them. From the Middle Ages onwards, London lawyers settled in areas of their own known as the Inns of Court. These settlements are still there, pullulating with solicitors and barristers. Perhaps because both sorts earn their living by talking, the places where

Regiments of roofs in Ealing mark the standard pattern of suburban London. Thousands of acres of country disappeared beneath houses like these, built between the wars—but Londoners, among the world's most avid flower-lovers, saved what was left for back-gardens.

they work are places of refreshing quiet. One of these legal quarters is called The Temple. It is an area that rouses every true Londoner's enthusiasm, so I shall let a supreme Londoner describe it.

"There are still worse places than The Temple", says Charles Dickens in *Barnaby Rudge*, "for basking in the sun, or resting idly in the shade. There is yet a drowsiness in its courts, and a dreamy dullness in its trees and gardens: those who pace its lanes and squares may yet hear the echoes of their footsteps on the sounding stones and read upon its gates in passing from the tumult of the Strand or Fleet Street, 'Who enters here leaves noise behind'. There is still the splash of falling water in fair Fountain Court . . . "

And so on. The alliteration has grown old-fashioned, but The Temple remains just as Dickens described it. There are two other lawyers' havens, Lincoln's Inn and Gray's Inn. But perhaps I should warn the stranger who has had enough of the "dreamy dullness" that, in spite of the names, there are no pubs in these places. Drinking is done, but only at the ritual dinners that all students must eat before they are "called to the Bar", again not a place of refreshment, but the ceremony of being made a "barrister", or superior sort of attorney. The point of The Temple and the Inns for a lover of London is that here he can walk or lounge for undisturbed hours by the London that the "Georgian" property developers made. One strolls through these sanctuaries full of admiration for those men, wishing we had more like them today.

The houses are in terraces, all of a rich brown brick, with oblong windows, their framework painted white. There is some decoration—a canopy over a door, for instance—but not too much of it. Narrow lanes lead from square to square, sometimes under arches. There are trees, those in Lincoln's Inn being magnificent and of great age. Flagstones serve for paving. Here and there rises a great hall, or a church. Nothing is written on the walls, save the name of the square and a number. Although we are in the heart of a great city, there are no advertisements. The plans are casual and confusing. Little maps are tucked away in unobtrusive corners to help you find your lawyer, which is as well, for the calm and quiet discourages one from asking a passer-by one's way. Often, there is no one to ask.

In a sense, this present tranquillity is deceptive; it is not quite in keeping with the period. Horses are noisy animals and carriages rattle. The London of the Georges and Queen Anne was not as peaceful as this. As well as the carriages there were street cries, which, though set to pretty tunes, could be ear-splitting—as those who, like myself, can remember from hearing the last of them before they were put down by law.

Not so peaceful even today are some of the other examples of this Georgian heritage. Queen Anne's Gate, in Westminster, perfectly preserved, is now a busier bottleneck than when it was built. More open, and still virtually unspoiled, is Bedford Square in Bloomsbury, a piece of land-

In residential districts of consequence such as Mayfair and Belgravia, the reserved uniformity of the wide, solid front doors, painted or varnished, is accented by doorknockers and handles that add a touch of individuality, usually in brilliantly polished brass of 18th- or 19th-Century design.

speculation by the dukes of Bedford. In Russell Square there is a monument to one of these dukes, surrounded by symbolic figures intent on impressing us (like all true gentlemen of the time) with the fact that his heart lay in the countryside and farming. (Maybe, but the family had a shrewd eye for a nice parcel of property.) Still, it is fair to say that in these great piazzas the nobles have left us, there is just a touch of country. In the middle of most of them are small parks, well-tended, with seats. Here, too, as Dickens noted, you can forget London, even at midday.

The developer, then as now, ate up London's countryside. In 1807 the poet Southey describes Portman Square as being "on the outskirts of the town, and approached on one side by a road unlit, unpaved, and inaccessible to carriages". Today it is as urban as one can conceive, surrounded by hotels, offices and modern blocks of flats. At some point since Southey's time another approach must have been provided for the carriages, for one of the delights of living in its stately houses was to have footmen leap from the carriages and thunder on the knocker of the door—the louder the noise the more distinguished the visitor.

The houses themselves deserve a moment's study because their peculiar construction set the fashion for the vast majority of good houses, and the style is preserved in London today. Anyone staying at a boarding house, or hiring lodgings at modest expense, will have to suffer all their inconveniences. They were built when servants were cheap; they have lasted until these times, when servants are unobtainable. The servants worked downstairs, in the basement; their mistresses and masters lived upstairs. Stairs—there were and are endless stairs. The rooms were large, but narrow, since land was expensive (or profits had to be high) and so the houses were packed in side by side.

The rooms were often decorated in a splendid style, with much panelling and gold leaf. Huge chimney pieces were a mark of rank. The better and more spacious houses (but still with endless stairs) were in Grosvenor Square, built by the nobles who attended on the monarch in near-by Buckingham Palace. Only foreign embassies can afford to keep up these mansions today. Getting a visa can often provide an opportunity for seeing what the inside of these houses once was like.

But to a Londoner like me, these squares and gardens are much more than pieces of history, or rather, they are part of that much more important history, my own. Here are the pavements which I walked as a young man with some chosen companion, talking, putting the world to rights. Here are the places in which I built, not Georgian houses, but castles in the air. Here the trees under which I sat in silence when my castles came tumbling down. Here are the places in which I strode, head up and with a lengthened step, after my first successes—an encouraging word from a publisher whose offices were behind a Grecian portico in one of the houses, or with a letter burning in my pocket that had arrived at my lodgings by the morning's post announcing that I had been accepted for my first real job in the real world.

For the Londoner, these places are like the café on Montparnasse to which the Parisian returns and sits in a corner, thinking of all the credit he ran up when he was young, or the dark little *trattoria* to which the Roman goes back and remembers how he poured out his youthful troubles to the *padrone* who assured him they would all seem less after a big plate of his wife's *spaghetti alla bolognese*—and they did.

And those stairs. As a young Londoner I climbed them, flight after flight, in the houses which had been turned into lodgings, Here were my garrets, although the landlady would have been outraged to hear them called so; I was always "the young gentleman in the Third Floor Back".

But I have described only the London, once beautiful, that is still in part there for us to saunter through, a London fit for Jane Austen or Anthony Trollope. What of Dickens' slums? A statistic takes us straight there. Between 1801 and 1840 (Queen Victoria came to the throne as a young girl in 1837) the population of London doubled. It rose from one million to two million in 40 years, and entirely altered the face of the city.

A new sort of property developer arose. To cope with an expanding population, we now pile box upon box until we have made one huge box which we call a block of flats. The builders of this new London put the boxes side by side and even back to back. London sprawled. It spread south to Southwark and Bermondsey, west to Pimlico, north to Islington and east to Whitechapel and Limehouse—the famous East End of London, which is contrasted bitterly by social reformers with the opulent West End (not an end at all but the centre of the metropolis). William Cobbett, a reformer of the early 19th Century with a gift for a telling phrase, called London "The Great Wen". These new suburbs soon degenerated because the developers did not keep the houses in repair and the inhabitants could not afford to. Thus arose the slums.

These slums provided Dickens with some of his best copy. They also provide us with London's biggest paradox: many of the slum-dwellers *liked* life in the slums. None of us outside the slums realized this until Hitler conceived the idea that if he bombed them, the inhabitants would rise in wrath against the Government. He had not read John Evelyn. Being Londoners, they did nothing of the sort. Once again, their stoicism was as much a wonder as the magnitude of the disaster.

Still, with the war ended, the slums could not be rebuilt in their old form. Something better had to take their place. And so the new, more commodious blocks of flats were built on their sites; green spaces, in however niggardly a fashion, were provided.

In New York, Chicago, Calcutta or Tokyo, such progress would be hailed with universal joy. It is not so in London. Louis Heren, deputy editor of that organ of the Establishment, *The Times*, was born and brought up in a slum. He wrote a book saying how much he enjoyed the experience and how sorry he is that he cannot repeat it. *The Times* printed long extracts from his book before publication, with large and approving headlines together with a touching photograph of Heren at an early age dressed in a Lord Fauntleroy suit and surrounded by his slum-dwelling family.

When a gifted writer publishes an autobiography, we all know it cannot be taken as unbiased evidence. But I can produce more. Before I embarked on this chapter, I visited the West End. There I saw an exhibition of contemporary paintings by an artist who had been born and bred in the East End. They were pictures of the slums. The title of the exhibition was "Say Goodbye! You may never See Them Again". The exhibition was so successful with Londoners, a book was later made on it, with the same title. It was a best-seller.

Why should people born in such appalling conditions be so nostalgic about them? In fact, they are quite voluble about it. Families I once knew as a boy to be living in destitution now have clean and commodious flats. They complain that instead of living side by side, which is what men have done since they inhabited rock-shelters, they live on top of one another, which is unnatural. Instead of having available the open friendliness of the streets they must meet in pubs, which are not by any means the cosy places that foreigners imagine them to be. The pub is an institution designed for profit—enormous profit; the street-corner was free. Besides, women generally do not like pubs, nor do they like their new environment. Instead of the backyard fence they have welfare centres, where civil servants are paid salaries to keep them happy, although the civil servants are noticeably un-jolly themselves.

Still, as a Londoner, I must be even-handed. Let the planners have their say in the person of an old friend. He was brought up in a slum near Wapping Docks. He worked as a lad in a City warehouse, and it was there I met him. I recently looked him up. He still lives in Wapping. He has a flat on the top floor of a block built after the bombing. He has a fine view of the Thames, and the great river looks particularly romantic in the evening when the lights come on. It was on one such romantic evening that he reminded me that in the house where he was born there were four storeys; they were occupied by six families, one of which lived five to a room. For all these families there was one lavatory, and one tap for water. Looking out at his view, he said, "Thank God my children never knew that."

So, by the end of this century, and perhaps before, London may have no slums, and its inhabitants may well know of them only from books. A great deal has been written about them, from Dickens onwards, for they made dramatic copy. Not much has been written about something much more typical of London, and which indeed makes up the greater part of it. I mean the suburbs.

London's suburbs are not quite like those of most other cities; I refer to the tidy towns in the countryside, within commuting distance of the metro-

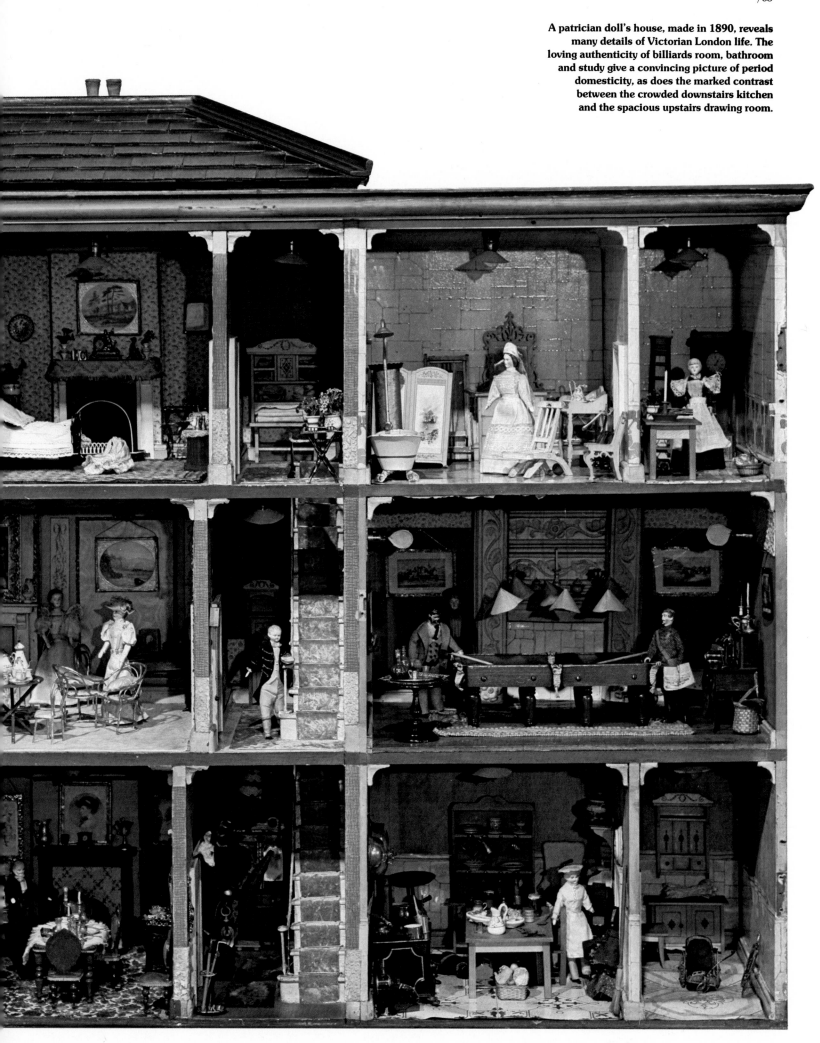

A patrician doll's house, made in 1890, reveals many details of Victorian London life. The loving authenticity of billiards room, bathroom and study give a convincing picture of period domesticity, as does the marked contrast between the crowded downstairs kitchen and the spacious upstairs drawing room.

polis. The Londoner refers to those suburbs as "the country". London's true suburbs, in turn, are what a New Yorker would call "greater London". And, as I shall explain, they are of two distinctly different types.

As The Great Wen expanded, London's property developers stopped building both squares and slums. There was money about, most of it belonging to people who had climbed the most slippery of all the rungs of the British social ladder, that between the lower middle class and the middle class. The broad middle class is always called the backbone of the nation. If that is so, we might describe the lower middle class as extending from the middle vertebrae to the coccyx. They are somewhat sat upon, but are considered indispensable. The point that concerns us is that, in the course of time, they prosper. Their small shops become big ones, the sons of tradesmen go into the professions or, nowadays, into politics and the Civil Service. In short, the lower middle classes better themselves.

Since nobody will admit to being lower middle class, it is impossible to say how many of them existed in London at any one period. But if the curious traveller will take a long drive out of central London he will form the impression that two or three generations ago the lower middle class comprised the majority of the population. That may have been the cause of Gladstone's celebrated advice to some foreigners: "The best way to see London, gentlemen, is from the top of a bus." Gladstone's advice appears particularly apt as soon as the traveller is clear of the centre. The bus enters an area consisting of row upon row of little houses; but the rows are different. One will have Tudor gables, like old London. Others will have classic pilasters slapped up on otherwise dull fronts. Others mysteriously go Dutch or even Hans Christian Andersen. They have nameboards hanging from porches so tiny that they barely give shelter to a dog. The names are those of royal palaces, celebrated country seats of the nobility or, more touchingly, of places where the owners spent their honeymoon. Like the houses of the poor, they share side walls with the neighbours. But they have upstairs lavatories and several taps. They all have front gardens. These may have lawns no bigger than a hearthrug, but they are a badge of respectability. The Queen of England would no more be seen swinging on the front gate of Buckingham Palace than would Mrs. Brown be seen doing the same thing at her "Sandringham" or "Balmoral".

These are what could be called the inner suburbs. Fine specimens of this London can be found in Streatham, Bromley and a dozen other places. It is best to stick firmly to Gladstone's advice and stay on the bus. To try to find a particular house, especially on a rainy day, can rapidly turn into a nightmare. But if you should try—and the house is found, the tiny front garden traversed, the chimes rung as one crouches under the portico, be assured that a warm welcome awaits you. The rooms will be small, the furniture too big, and you must guard against sitting on the cat. But it is all wonderfully cosy. The overwhelming impression that the

An authentic Victorian interior lies behind stained-glass drawing-room windows of a house in Stafford Terrace, Kensington. Once the home of Linley Sambourne, a widely-travelled artist and Punch cartoonist, it has been lived in quite unchanged by his family, and its crowded surfaces perfectly record the taste of the time.

inhabitants of these architectural pot-pourris give you is that they want nothing better in the world.

It is quite wrong. They are wracked with ambition. They want to detach themselves from their neighbours with the passion that one imagines animates Siamese twins. They want a house that stands by itself, well away from the road behind a big front garden, with another garden at the back. They want a tree or two, and tea on the lawn. They want roses. They want, in short, a house in what could be called the outer suburbs, farther out from The Great Wen. Not, be it noted, too far out. That comes later, when they have moved one step more up the ladder, to the upper middle class. Then they can go to "the country", and enter the world of the Country Club, which, since it does not belong to London, will not concern us here.

From the time of Victoria's Diamond Jubilee down to our day, the property developers have been happy to oblige. Having built the semi-detached, they went on to build the splendidly detached. Thus London's second, outer ring of suburbs arose. The older examples of these houses have mellowed with time; they give London a charm not to be found in the environs of Paris or Rome or Madrid or many other ancient cities.

A fine specimen of these can be reached by a very short ride on Gladstone's recommended bus-top. One goes along Kensington High Street, as nondescript and dull a highway as could be imagined. Dismount, and take a brief walk up Campden Hill, which seems to lead to nowhere in particular. Suddenly you are in Holland Park. It bursts upon you with the surprise of foreign travel. It scarcely seems part of London, and it certainly has nothing to do with the noisy, garish High Street you have just left. It is quiet, almost as quiet as The Temple. It is set about with attractive houses, but the overwhelming impression is of trees. It is as though the central greenery of the Georgian squares had been enlarged, and the houses built, not round it, but in it.

In a sense, this is true. Holland Park was once the grounds of Holland House. This was the imposing home of a noble family. Byron and

Macaulay frequented its salons, but bombing and restoration have left little of the house itself. But the houses around it, built by prosperous middle-class Victorians, make up for this loss. Their exuberant architecture shouts to be noticed, like the Lord Mayor of London's mace sticking out of the coach window. These are houses built by men who wanted you to know they had *arrived*. Here is no question of following French or Italian taste. One seems to hear the voice of the men who ordered these buildings telling the architect that any damn' style would do as long as it looked like money. The trees, the flowering shrubs, the gardens that surround them serve a similar purpose. Observing much the same thing in America, Thorsten Veblen, in a learned monograph, wrote of "conspicuous consumption and expenditure". Those London magnates would have considered the adjective unnecessary: *of course* it was conspicuous. What else?

If these millionaires were way up the backbone of the nation, adroit men could climb on their shoulders. The great new houses needed furnishing. They needed pictures, not only portraits of the owners and their families, but Art. The owners did not know much about Art, but they knew what they liked, and that was yards of canvas covered by some painter who was widely known to have the nerve to charge enormous fees.

One such painter was Frederick Leighton. He painted historical subjects, a shrewd choice for patrons who had everything except a history. More shrewdly still, he chose subjects that included partially draped women— "The Bath of Psyche" for instance—which was a lot easier for the million-aire to understand than chiaroscuro and perspective. Leighton had a deserved success: he became as rich as his employers, and even went one better than a lot of them. He got himself made a peer of the realm. It followed that he would build his own house in Holland Park. It is in such supernaturally bad taste that succeeding generations have left it untouched, inside and out, no doubt from awe. Now a museum, it should not be missed.

I will not attempt to describe Lord Leighton's High Victorian paintings. I shall merely report that, having examined them at length in Leighton

Chelsea's Floral Glory

For one festive week in May, passionate gardeners from city and suburbs flock to the grounds of the Royal Hospital in Chelsea, which suddenly burgeon with the Royal Horticultural Society's biggest flower show of the year. Inside the huge marquee, where aisles of glowing flowers stretch away in every direction, the most eloquent of flower-show gestures is made again and again, as visitors lean down with half-closed eyes to sniff the new varieties of roses making their debut.

House, I was about to leave when one of the uniformed attendants delayed me at the exit and sought my opinion. I was at a loss for words, but he was not. For the next 15 minutes he told me, with fervour, what he suffered through being locked up, day after day, with Lord Leighton's productions. Pathetically, he told me that he had taken the job only because he had liked pictures since he was a little boy.

I shall, however, briefly describe the house. Every inch of the interior is loaded with decoration. This was very much in the taste of the newly rich. The profusion pleased them, as it would have pleased Cecil B. De Mille, director of some of Hollywood's most extravagantly tasteless productions (De Mille himself began his career in the fur trade). Every artistic style is represented, for Victorians were as broadminded in their aesthetic preferences as Field-Marshal Hermann Goering. Leighton, however, surpassed even him. The central room is a domed courtyard lined with Moorish tiles. A Moorish fountain plays in the centre. There is no record that Lord Leighton smoked hashish or kept a harem. The only point of this oriental extravaganza was that it cost a great deal. Haroun el Rashid had a lot of money, and so did the Victorians. They even had chamber pots made of solid silver; some had two handles, so that they could be used for holding flowers. (One such survives among the ceremonial plate of the Lord Mayor of York, that other British city of self-made men.)

To state it simply, the Victorian age was given to gross exaggeration, from the Queen's heavily underlined letters to an Empire too big to be properly governed. The Boer Wars after the turn of the century sobered things down. The British in South Africa had been all but defeated by a handful of Dutch farmers, and the more thoughtful among them realized that the day of Nelson, Wellington, Clive and similar heroes was over. The middle classes grew less ostentatious, and concentrated more on comfort than display. Silver chamber pots gave way to indoor plumbing, a revolution that impressed the French to such a degree that they still use the prim English initials to describe the convenience: W.C., for "water closet". Interior decoration followed this practical trend: it grew less crowded and much less ornate. The houses followed suit. Architects returned to the Georgian notion of restraint. "Neo-Georgian", an imitation of the bygone style, became the fashion. The imitations were often remarkably good for the exteriors, and even better than the originals inside. There were fewer stairs because there were fewer servants.

The suburbs spread. The trees and shrubs flourished until whole streets looked like parks. They are still to be found, in Richmond, Wimbledon, Sydenham, and many other places. The houses, too big for modern families, have been sought by institutions such as schools; consequently the gardens have been tended with loving care. To explore these areas, in spring or autumn, is a special London pleasure. Sunday morning is the best time, when the remaining home owners walk their dogs, expensive varieties of this animal having replaced the previous cats. It is a Londoner's foible to take pride in being able to recognize the breed of the dogs, and a visitor from the Continent does well to master this art. If he is able to distinguish a setter from a spaniel, or, even better, spot a touch of one in the other, the Londoner will make him doubly welcome. When he is taken home to one of the splendidly detached houses for Sunday dinner (eaten about 2 p.m.), he will be allowed to mangle English grammar as much as he pleases.

The bosky, flower-deep suburbs, both Victorian and Neo-Georgian, have suffered from the vagaries of public taste. From being the Nirvana of all successful middle-class people, they fell into disrepute in the 1920s. The *upper* middle classes derided the life that was lived in them. The distinction between this section of the population and the middle classes is too subtle to be properly explained in words. It has to be learned from long experience, and I suggest that the foreigner practice distinguishing dogs until his sensibilities are suitably refined. But there was a time when the mere mention of the name of a suburb could bring a delighted laugh from theatre audiences in the West End.

All that has changed. The upper middle classes, hard pressed by the loss of Empire and the incomes they derived from it, have now begun to look upon these outer-ring suburbs as monuments to England's vanished prosperity. Life in its panelled lounges and in its wide gardens is now seen to have merit. A poet with a gift for rhyme, John Betjeman, was the first to give tongue to this change in attitude, and his celebration of the suburbs became so popular that he was rewarded with a knighthood and the post of Poet-Laureate. He and his admirers became active in trying to preserve the suburbs from destruction at the hands of the developers. The older suburbs are fast becoming a new subject for nostalgia. But, then, as we have seen, the Londoner can grow nostalgic about almost anything. It is the other side of the medal of his willingness to accept change. Besides, it pays off. Lord Leighton and his followers, for example, found new admirers when the Arab oil sheikhs bought up Victorian art at very satisfactory prices. There is always someone who is newly rich.

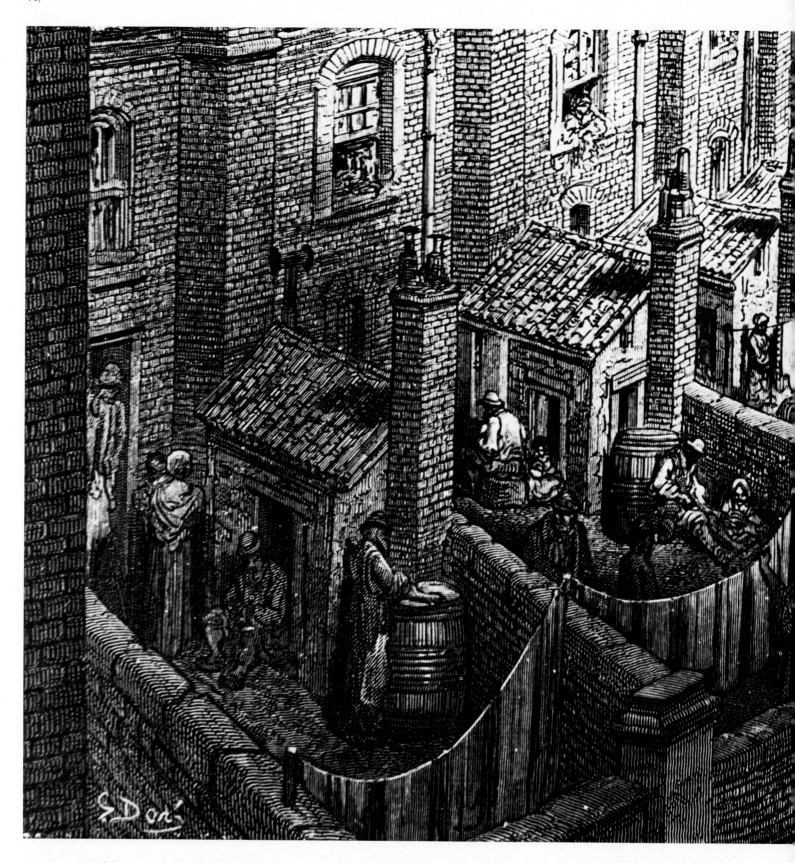

"London in the Quick"

Doré's engravings of workers' walled-off back yards showed how Londoners, in their search for open air and privacy, lived in endless rows of people-pens.

London, like other great cities, has attracted its share of talented artists, and among them was the famous French illustrator, Gustave Doré. In 1869 he began a series of engravings of the city that took three years to finish. "Our plan", said writer Blanchard Jerrold who collaborated on the publication of his engravings, "is to present London in the quick to the reader—as completely as we may be able to grasp the

prodigious giant . . . " Although Doré was lionized by English society (even Queen Victoria asked him to call), he found his most powerful stimulus where the city was darkest, dirtiest and most crowded. He rarely sketched on the spot, trusting the "photographs in my head". While this method led to some errors, it enabled Doré to distil the essence of Victorian London and preserve it forever in his engravings.

Billingsgate's wholesale business took place in auction rooms, like this one at right, in the early hours while most of London was asleep. Doré delighted in packing such scenes with "types" of British faces he stored in his mind.

Not only at Billingsgate but in most of London's 40 street markets a shopper could pause to down a snack of fresh oysters from the shell. Often as cheap as a farthing each, oysters were a staple of a working man's diet.

Doré, Jerrold wrote, found the daily opening of Billingsgate fish market (left) "one of those picturesque tumults which delight the artist's eye". Here, before dawn, bummarees—fish salesmen—buyers and fish crowd Dark House Lane, at the heart of the Thameside market.

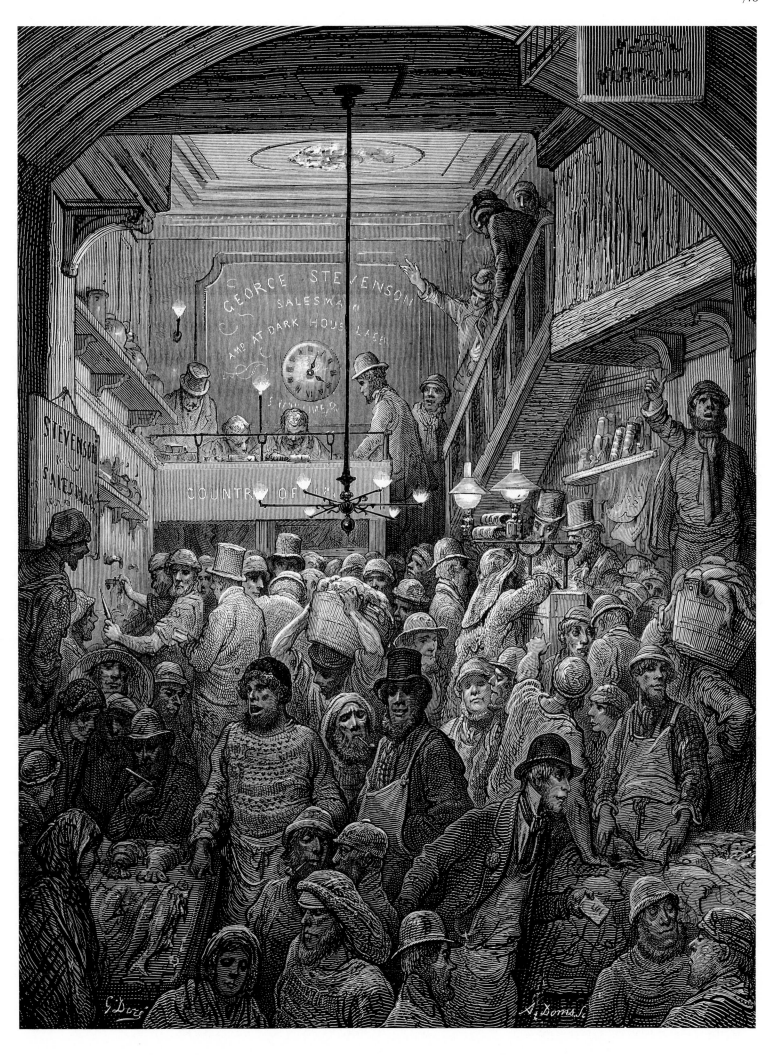

London's variety of street traders, like this
hardware dealer, fascinated the French artist.

Because oranges were a cheap commodity, some
4,000 hawkers peddled them on the streets.

The poor bought almost all their needs,
including these matches, from street vendors.

"The best drink out," sang the ginger beer man.
He added ice to keep up with a new fashion.

"Lemonade" made from chemicals and lemon
flavour was sold by pedlars from portable tubs.

A flypaper merchant carried his own advertisement
—an insect-covered sample on his hat.

Doré mistakenly pictured Cockney flower girls
selling posies from French-style baskets.

Poor Londoners, such as this dog seller,
dressed as ragged imitations of the rich.

The pathos of London's homeless moved the
artist to some of his most effective work. In
this gas-lit scene men are compelled to bath
under supervision before being given a bed
in a charity-sponsored "night-refuge".

Before sleeping, homeless men hear Bible
readings, "comforting, let us hope, many of
the aching heads". Doré felt a kinship with
Dickens and in such scenes touched Victorian
hearts and consciences in much the same way.

Pannemaker-Doms Sc

4

Pomp and Circumstance

I am no good at all at making up bed-time stories for the young. When I find myself having to do so with no escape, I fall back on the tale of Poor Claude. It is politely received, although I am aware that I am considered somewhat less than A. A. Milne or Tolkien. The story tells of a very respectable stockbroker in the City of London who all his life wished he could dress up in those magnificent clothes that they wore in the Middle Ages, and walk in a royal procession to the sound of trumpets. All his City friends would be there to watch him, and they would take the whole thing seriously. In my bed-time story, Claude's dream came true. In real life, it did not; that is why his friends called him Poor Claude.

Poor Claude was not really poor. He was a partner in one of those City firms with oak-panelled offices and polished calling-bells that I have described. He had all the money he needed, together with a pleasant house, a devoted housekeeper and a manservant who served delicious meals. He also had a sideboard with massy silver plate. Claude was perfectly content, save for one thing. He wanted to be Blue Mantle. Blue Mantle wore that splendid dress right out of the Middle Ages and he walked, at least once a year, in a royal procession, to the sound of trumpets.

Unfortunately for Poor Claude, there could be only one Blue Mantle at a time in the whole Kingdom. But Blue Mantles are not immortal. Poor Claude was certain that when one of them died he would be the next on to whose shoulders the Mantle would fall. He had reason. Among his friends were such people as Norroy and Ulster King-at-Arms, Lancaster Herald, Rouge Dragon, Portcullis, and Blue Mantle himself, names that came from the heralds who surrounded English monarchs from the Middle Ages, and who still do. They often dined with Poor Claude and they dined very well, because Claude's devoted housekeeper knew that Rouge Dragon liked his beef underdone and Norroy and Ulster King-at-Arms had to keep off sugary things. In spite of this, when Blue Mantle died, his role fell on other shoulders, and Poor Claude lived unhappily ever after.

Should you think I have made all this up, I must ask you to go to a house in London, ten minutes walk from Cheapside, where you will find the names of these persons written on doors, in large white letters. If you are lucky, some of these doors will be opened for you. Behind them you will find not only Norroy and Ulster King-at-Arms, but his companions Garter King-at-Arms and Clarenceux. Their assistants, the Heralds, may not be at home, but you can ask for them; their names are Somerset Herald, Richmond Herald, together with Lancaster, Windsor, Chester and York,

By Horse Guards Parade, former members of a regiment of Foot Guards can still demonstrate a creditable standard of precision marching. Their bowlers and tightly-furled umbrellas, worn for a Remembrance Day parade, are as much a uniform for them as the scarlet tunics or battledress they wore in the Service.

all Heralds. On occasion you might also meet the helpers of these mightily named: the Pursuivants, or followers—Rouge Croix, Rouge Dragon, Portcullis and Blue Mantle. If you do, Norroy will not greet you armed cap-a-pie; he will wear a business suit. Rouge Dragon will not breathe fire; he will be the most reluctant dragon you have ever met, with charming manners and no wish in the world to do you harm. Portcullis will not greet you with boiling oil. They are all very nice gentlemen and they could exist nowhere in the world but London. They are a part of that lore of occasional pomp and circumstance which marks London in the eyes of the world, and rightly so.

The place is the College of Arms. It is in Queen Victoria Street, but the taxi-driver had better be directed to the College of Heralds, for that is the name by which it is known to Londoners. The College was designed by Sir Christopher Wren. Since he was an architect who could build in any style, he could well have run up a medieval castle, but in fact it is the sober and harmonious style of house of the 17th Century. Inside is an entrance hall panelled in gleaming wood, and it is awesomely beautiful. To get beyond the hall you must state your business, and this can be only one thing: you must believe that an English monarch had at some time given an ancestor of yours the right to armorial bearings, a shield, that is (or an "escutcheon") on which were displayed various symbols, lines, balls and improbable animals. On top of this was a helmet which, to the knowledgeable, reveals your rank. A mere knight has a simple helmet; a duke one that is very grand. Norroy, Garter and Clarenceux will, after a long delay and a fee, tell you whether you have a right to bearings or not. If their word is "No", and you still display the bearings in your drawing room, you are merely a snob. For a further fee, they will design your personal escutcheon, which will often include a reference to your name. Persons who have got thus far should be warned the Middle Ages had a taste for atrocious puns, and the taste survives in the College of Arms, especially when they think up Latin mottoes.

We live in an egalitarian age. It might be thought that the College is a preposterous institution in these times. It is not. Norroy and Ulster King-at-Arms might regretfully inform you that your only traceable ancestor was hanged for sheep stealing, but your money will not have been wasted. The records of the College of Arms are invaluable to a historian; and they are preserved with a loving care that is not always lavished on historical documents. Besides, a desire to be well-descended can arise in the most unlikely breasts. America is the bastion of democracy where all men are equal and none may display any symbol of his status except his credit card. The College of Arms is approached through a magnificent pair of iron gates. They are the gift of a grateful American.

Besides, these men have another, more important, function. London is famous for the pageantry that surrounds the monarch. Its colour, its dignity, and above all its timing, are the despair of such foreign monarchs as are left, including those perennial monarchs in the Vatican, the Popes.

On royal occasions in London things always go right. To show how remarkable that is, let me describe some ceremonials that did not.

I have observed three Popes, at length and on their own ground, which is St. Peter's. Everybody knows that the ceremonial inside and outside St. Peter's is very grand and elaborate. There is also a lot of it, year in and year out. It is organized by a functionary called the Vicar-General. He has the rank of an archbishop, but that does not save him from being a very harassed man. His office is a small room in the Vatican Palace that you enter by walking through a large fresco, provided someone is there to show you which is a real door and which a painted one. The problems the Vicar-General faces behind it are no less unusual.

For instance, Pope Pius XII was utterly devoted to his task, but he very much disliked long religious ceremonies. The result was that nobody in the Vatican could be quite sure in advance whether he would sing Pontifical High Mass or not. I was assured on one occasion by the Vicar-General that he would, and the Pope did not turn up. On the other hand, attending a beatification of some holy person at which I was firmly told he would not

Sturdy mounts for the Household Cavalry's massive kettle drums are hard to find. A tradition that they should be patchy piebald or skewbald makes the search more difficult. This one, Cicero, was pulling carts in Edinburgh when the Queen herself saw him and passed on word of a new candidate for the job.

The Royal Touch

London is a royal city, the home of Britain's sovereign, and everywhere are signs of its connection with monarchy. Crowns and regal emblems appear on buildings, banners, lamps and all conceivable materials, from the sparkling brass of a cavalry bridle and the embroidered cloth of a Beefeater's tunic (both bottom row), to the polished wood of a Home Office door (top row left) and the punched metal of a Post Office telephone box (middle row).

Sometimes the crown is part of the arresting brilliance of pageantry, as on a trumpeter's banner (top row second from left); sometimes part of the architectural grace that sovereigns have bestowed on walls and gates of their city; and sometimes it is part of the Royal Coat of Arms shops are entitled to put up if they have been honoured by royal custom (top row centre, middle row left).

BY APPOINTMENT TO HIS LATE MAJESTY KING GEORGE VI
FINE ART PUBLISHERS THOS AGNEW & SONS LTD LONDON

attend, he came in right at the end of the ceremony, to delirious cheers from the congregation. Again, the Pope wears a crown called the tiara. There are rules about when he should and when he should not, but they are not much help to the Vicar-General. John XXIII liked wearing a tiara. Paul VI wore it only once, and then he gave it away. Paul VI early gained a reputation for being punctual: John XXIII was so late for his coronation that we in St. Peter's decided that he was about to make history by giving up the whole idea. He arrived in due course, carried on his portable throne, looking sea-sick (because, as he said later, he *was* sea-sick).

With such changeable masters, it is no wonder that the Vicar-General sometimes gets his wires crossed. My most treasured memory was of an elaborate ceremonial involving both the Greek Uniate Rite and the Catholic Rite. Witnessing this at close quarters, I heard Paul VI say at one point, in an irritated voice, "Well, do I *say* it or *sing* it?" For some long and breathless moments, nobody could tell him.

Such accidents could not have happened with the British Monarchy, and this is due to the College of Heralds. They bring their vast knowledge of royal etiquette to the service of a functionary called the Earl Marshal. He is not a member of the College, but his word is law, even to royalty. By tradition, the Earl Marshal is the Duke of Norfolk. By tradition, too, the dukes of Norfolk are not loquacious. They say what is to be done, and that is that. One Earl Marshal decreed that, for the Investiture of Prince Charles as Prince of Wales, there should be one rather limited shelter and everybody else should be in the open. When someone asked him what would happen if it rained, His Grace replied, "We shall all get very wet".

Once a year the Earl Marshal and his Heralds organize one of the most significant ceremonies in England's history. It is the opening of a new session of Parliament by the monarch. The uniforms are resplendent, especially those of the Heralds. Each consists in the main of a sort of jacket known as a tabard. It is embroidered with the Royal Arms, and it does not belong to them. It costs a lot of money (in the 1960s it cost over £400) and the monarch foots the tailoring bill. Nowadays, the Heralds, on retiring from their posts, thriftily hand their tabards on to their successors; some of the older tabards are darned. As well as the great Heralds I have named, there are others with the resounding title of Heralds Extraordinary. This merely means they are not on the royal pay-roll. That is, they do it for fun, as Poor Claude would willingly have done. One of them told me quite frankly that he enjoyed dressing up.

The monarch drives to the Houses of Parliament in a state coach. It looks like the coronation coach but is not; like the Pope's portable throne, the coronation coach sways so much it makes its occupants sea-sick. This "Irish Coach", as it is called, is better sprung. Otherwise the procession is exactly the same as the coronation procession, which people pay large sums to see. The Opening of Parliament draws much smaller crowds and

Like a single organism a detachment of Foot Guards turns sharp right out of the Mall towards Horse Guards Parade, during a rehearsal for Trooping the Colour. This annual military review, a brilliantly-coloured spectacle watched by many thousands, is performed with precision and flawless timing.

the knowledgeable Londoner can stroll up at the last moment and see everything. On one particularly raw morning, I took a visitor to witness it. He was overjoyed to receive a special personal salute from Queen Elizabeth II, there being only a handful of people on that very windy corner.

On arrival at the Houses of Parliament (known as the Palace of Westminster, although it is not a palace and the monarch does not own it) the ruler retires, is robed, and puts on the crown. This is the most expensive hat in the history of haberdashery, particularly as it will be worn only on this one day each year. (There are two other occasions: one is the coronation, the other more sombre. It does not help the difficult task of balancing it for a monarch to know that when he dies it will be put on his or her coffin.)

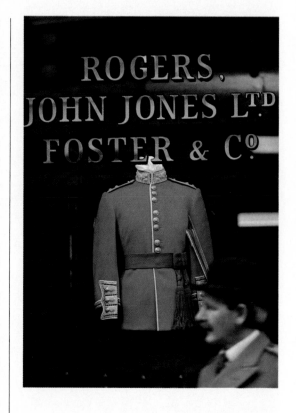

Surrounded by the great Officers of State and preceded by the Heralds, the monarch now moves in procession to the House of Lords. Before him is carried, on a cushion, the Cape of Maintenance, a velvet affair the significance of which escapes everybody except, presumably, the College of Heralds, and a four-foot long Sword of State. This is very heavy. It is carried by a field-marshal who is customarily quite elderly. Field-Marshal Montgomery once nearly dropped it, but one of the Earl Marshal's minions got to him in the nick of time.

The House of Lords is filled with peers. Each wears an ermine-edged robe and a coronet. The coronet is of silver-gilt, and is decorated with balls. The more balls, the lower the rank of the peer. It might be wondered how, in an impoverished Britain, people can afford to have such an expensive garb in their wardrobes. The answer is that they are mainly hired from a firm of tailors called Moss Brothers (written "Moss Bros." and among peers pronounced "mossbross") who thus play a humble but essential part in upholding the British Constitution.

The monarch now takes his seat upon the throne, the Queen or the Consort sitting on a similar seat. A functionary called Black Rod, a gentleman in kneebreeches, is sent to the House of Commons to summon the Members. Once arrived, he must knock on the door with his rod. He does this three times before he is admitted. This is to show that the Commons are not at the beck and call of the monarch. The Members of the Commons now walk informally to the House of Lords, and there royalty gets its own back—there is not enough room for all of them, so they have to stand in a huddle, some of them in the corridor.

The monarch then reads the Speech from the Throne. It is written for him by the government of the day and outlines their proposed legislation. Everyone knows what is in it, so it is not listened to with great attention. Edward VII once bet that he could say "mumble-bumble-bumble" in the middle of it and no-one would notice. He is said to have won. Since the invention of broadcasting, however, the Speech is read more audibly. But it must be read with an expressionless face and without emphasis. Monarchs vary in their elocution. Queen Elizabeth learned to perform

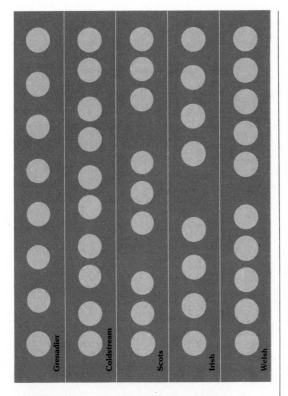

A crisply tailored Guards tunic glows scarlet in the window of a military outfitter's (left). The brass buttons spaced in threes mark it as a Scots Guards uniform. Tradition has given each Guards regiment its own button-spacing as an aid to identification. Some of them are labelled in the diagram above.

admirably, quite early in her reign, adopting the even tones of a head-mistress announcing the year's prizewinners.

How does London look upon its sovereign? To judge from the crowds that appear on television, London would seem to be royalist to a man. That is not quite true. The crowds are largely made up of provincials who have come to town for a spree and who have picked a royal occasion because it is a free show. The true Londoners have always looked upon the reigning monarch with a more measured gaze. They are loyal subjects, but any attempt to beat up excessive enthusiasm for the Royal Family falls flat. The most marked example of this was when King Edward VIII was on the verge of being pushed off the throne because he wanted to marry the American lady who later became the Duchess of Windsor. Loudspeaker vans toured the streets urging the citizens to Stand By the King. London merely stood by.

There has long been more than a touch of republicanism in the Londoner. Here, for instance, is an extract from a London journal, *Reynolds' Newspaper*, for 19th June, 1887, just before Queen Victoria celebrated her Jubilee:

"Will any flunkey in Christendom tell us one good thing that the Queen, her sons and daughters or any of her inexhaustible brood of pauper relations 'made in Germany', has ever done for the people of this land? At Westminster Abbey next Tuesday, ten thousand persons (will be seen) all blasphemously falling down and worshipping a pampered old woman of sullen visage and sordid mind, because she is supposed to have in her veins some of the tainted fluid which coursed in the veins of that devotee of Sodom and Gomorrah, James I! Think of it, just Heavens!"

Such sentiments would no longer be found in the British Press, but they can be heard in many London pubs on and after some royal occasion. Even in the newspapers, they have their gentler echo. A considerable effort in public relations was made in 1973 to arouse some enthusiasm for the wedding of the Queen's daughter, Anne, to a personable young man of non-royal origin. The Princess was known to be much given to riding horses. On the day of the wedding a popular newspaper published across five columns a cartoon showing the royal coach and its team of horses. The Queen was shown putting her head out of the window and saying in reproof, "Anne!!"—to the bride, who was enthusiastically riding one of the horses. If the Queen, like her ancestor, was not amused, London was.

This wary coolness between the sovereign and the capital city is well shown in the matter of the royal surname. The monarch belongs to the House of Saxe-Coburg and Gotha, and for a while the name was used with pride. It is very German and so it should be. The family is of German origin. Victoria spoke fluent German to Albert, and her son Edward VII had a heavy German accent. *His* son, George V, was an honorary field-

The grey greatcoats worn by soldiers of the Foot Guards are part of their winter uniform. Their weighty bearskin caps are used summer and winter alike.

In scarlet summer coats the Chelsea Pensioners—retired soldiers of impeccable record—doff their tricorns to the Queen at their annual Founder's Day review.

marshal of the German army, and when in Berlin wore the uniform.

Then came the First World War. London had suffered the shock of aerial bombardment, and there was a widespread suspicion that spies were operating in and around the city, guiding the bombers to their targets by flashing lights. Demonstrations against people with German names took place, and the demand arose that the Royal Family change their name. Anonymous letters began to pour into Buckingham Palace, while people drew marked attention to the fact that the King had cousins living in England with names like Gleichen, Schleswig-Holstein and Battenberg.

The Prime Minister, David Lloyd George, thought that something should be done. The College of Heralds was consulted. The Heralds dug into their records and emerged with the none-too-happy news that a case could be made for the King belonging to the House of Wettin. Given the notoriously coarse sense of humour of the London Cockney, the range of possible witticisms on this particular name was daunting.

The Court put its thinking cap on. Someone suggested Fitzroy, meaning son of the king; but someone else pointed out that Charles II had used it to christen his bastards. "York", "Lancaster", "Plantagenet" were all suggested but turned down for various reasons by the Heralds. No-one, be it noted, suggested "the House of London".

Finally the King's private secretary, off the top of his head, suggested "the House of Windsor". Windsor is a provincial town with no royal connection save that it contains one of the country residences of the monarchs. It was adopted with relief.

The story does not quite end there. In 1947 Princess Elizabeth married a naval officer, Philip Mountbatten. He was made a British Prince; but because of memories of another consort, Prince Albert, who was never popular, Philip was also made a duke—not, again be it noted, the Duke of London (which would have been logical) but of Edinburgh. Philip, of course, was not at all Scots, and indeed on the first occasion of his wearing a kilt, had humorously curtsied to his father-in-law. His trials continued, for he found himself in the position of being a father who could not pass his name to his own son. The Queen put this right (or half-right) by decreeing in 1960 that in future the family's name should be "Mountbatten-Windsor". But "Mountbatten" is the mask contrived during the First World War for the family of the Battenbergs. So the Germans are back again. This would have pleased Kaiser Wilhelm II. On hearing of the change of name to "Windsor" he was much annoyed. He announced sarcastically to his courtiers that he was going to see a play by Shakespeare called *The Merry Wives of Saxe-Coburg and Gotha.*

This uneasiness about a surname is reflected in a similar uneasiness when the monarch deals with the Londoner. For most of this century it was a principle of the Royal Family that they should surround themselves with a certain air of mystery. The notion was that the public face of the monarchy should be given the maximum of exposure while, simultaneously, their private lives should be as private as possible. The scheme is excellent, but only one person has ever managed to carry it off successfully, and that is Greto Garbo. The Royal Family are less fortunate: so far from giving the impression that they wish to be alone, they appear to be gregarious to a fault. Apart from their monarchial duties of opening innumerable institutions and presiding at banquets, they also attend sporting events, visit the theatre, frequent night-spots, fall in and out of love, marry, produce children, at the same time managing to keep up an intense family life of reunions, birthdays, and so forth. Their doings are chronicled daily in *The Times* under the heading "Court Circular" and this is so packed with events it sometimes gives the impression that they are running for elective office.

At the same time, the air of mystery is fitfully maintained. Buckingham Palace, the London centre of all this activity, is rigidly closed to the public. The White House in Washington D.C. (or at least the ground floor) is open at certain hours to all. The Vatican may be visited by those who ask in advance. The Londoner who wishes to see inside one of his chief monuments is refused. Under pressure, an annex has been opened where a selection of pictures are temporarily displayed, after which they once more disappear. The loyal subject is, however, welcome to inspect the royal stables. This secretiveness has some comic results. The monarch awards knighthoods and decorations at investitures. I myself am undecorated, but several of my friends have been honoured. They complain that on this memorable occasion they are lined up like schoolboys, dubbed or be-medalled, and rapidly dismissed. Photographers being banned from under the roof, the fortunate congregate in the courtyard where they are portrayed holding their decorations shyly in their hands. As for the time-honoured ceremony of presentation at Court, this has been supplanted by a Garden Party: the monarch moves among the guests, a few of whom are presented; the rest, in the words of Shakespeare, must settle for being flattered by the sovereign eye.

The monarch's technique of mysteriousness extends to his dealings with the highest in the Land. Harold Wilson has recorded how, on being summoned to the ancient ceremony of kissing the monarch's hand on receiving the seals of office, he found to his surprise that kissing was out. Nobody, it appears, had told him.

The remoteness, at one stage, began to irritate first the Press and then the public. Royal permission was therefore granted for a film to be shot showing the Royal Family at home, the aim being to demonstrate that they were really just like ordinary people. The film certainly proved that the richest woman in the land (and possibly in the world) did not come down to breakfast smothered in diamonds. But it did little to allay the discontent of the British taxpayer, who is inclined to think that a Head of State who needs a subsidy of over one million pounds a year is a luxury that a country in economic decline can ill afford.

It would be easy to jump to the conclusion from all this that the British monarchy is on its last legs. On the contrary, in all probability its lease on life has been indefinitely prolonged. Constitutionally, the King can do no wrong; but he can do no right either. He must not interfere in the running of the country. The voters elect the Members of Parliament, according to their party programmes. The head of the winning party goes to the monarch and, in theory, is made Prime Minister, the sovereign having no choice in the matter. In practice, it does not always turn out that way.

In 1931 the country was governed by a Socialist Prime Minister, Ramsay MacDonald. An economic crisis hit the land. MacDonald, without consulting the major section of his party, suggested to King George V that he form a coalition with the Conservative opposition. The King, who liked MacDonald, agreed. The coalition was formed, to the astonishment of most of MacDonald's Socialist colleagues who were driven into the wilderness for decades. The country accepted the *fait accompli*, but in London it was the opinion of many of those in the know that the King had acted unconstitutionally. This view still persists. Nearer to our own times, a situation arose where there was more than one candidate to succeed the Prime Minister, who was on the point of resigning, because of illness and other unfavourable factors. Queen Elizabeth visited him in hospital and took his personal advice in the matter. She appointed Sir Alec Douglas-Home. Again, was the monarchy being strictly neutral, or was it using its position to interfere in the affairs of the country? If the latter, was it a bad thing?

Maybe not. Britain is no longer a great power. Its politics have lost the assurance of the old days. Coalitions of opposing parties may be a necessity in the future, and for a long time in the future. A monarch who can remain above the cockpit of the House of Commons may well be a political asset in a time of crisis. This is especially true if the sovereign has ruled for many years. His experience of affairs could be greater than that of any of the contenders for power.

When the monarch is crowned in Westminster Abbey, at the exact moment when the crown is placed on his head, the Abbey bells ring out and cannons boom over London. It is a sound which makes one's thoughts rove back over the centuries. For a while, at least, it seems that all the pomp and circumstance is something greater than a pageant arranged with such meticulous precision by the Earl Marshal and Heralds in their fine array. And to the Londoner, in a sense, it is.

The Life of a Cavalryman

Exercising his horse in Hyde Park, Trooper Clarke gallops past his barracks. His khaki uniform is a far cry from the resplendent one he wears when on duty.

London is a city that offers two ways for a young man to thunder through Hyde Park astride a costly, Irish-bred horse. One way is to be wealthy; the other, to be one of the Queen's Household Cavalry. As a child, Mike Clarke (above), son of a London shopkeeper, often watched the splendidly uniformed horsemen and uttered the wish of a thousand other English boys: to be one of them. By 16 he was. But the life of a cavalryman, he now knows, is not all galloping for pleasure or parading past Buckingham Palace. The troopers also serve in modern armoured units and spend long hours tending their horses and kit. Clarke pays a high toll in hard work before he dons the uniform and plumed helmet that transform the lean, fresh-faced 20-year-old into one of those grandly colourful symbols of Britain who are admired in their Whitehall sentry boxes.

High above Knightsbridge, Clarke inspects his mare, Ocarina, on a terrace of the modern barracks. He spends two hours a day grooming her, with special attention to her hoofs. Even though the horses have extra-heavy shoes for hard roads, they must be re-shod every month.

Polishing jackboots is an endless job. "When you see us walking all funny and stiff-legged," says Clarke, "it's only so we don't crease the boot-leather."

Donning a uniform and accessories weighing 49 pounds requires considerable help from a fellow dutyman.

Getting a last brush-up, troopers prepare for inspection. Clarke stands second in line from the right.

The Best-Groomed Men in London

Clarke can spend up to five hours a day cleaning equipment, half that time on his horse's tack and half on his own kit. His helmet, sword and breastplate must gleam like mirrors if a trooper is to rank high at inspection and win a coveted spot on the day's roster, such as first shift in the Number One sentry box. Over the years, equipment is passed from soldier to soldier; one of Clarke's boots, patched and mended, dates from 1916, the other from 1929.

London cabbies wait respectfully as a detachment of Blues and Royals, Clarke's regiment, clops across the Mall towards Whitehall where it will relieve the guard of the Life Guards, the other regiment in the Household Cavalry. Every day the one-and-a-half mile ride from the barracks to Whitehall is timed so that the cavalrymen pass Buckingham Palace while the Foot Guards are changing the guard there. Thus the Queen never goes unprotected during the changeover.

HGX 906K

During their hour-long stints, man and horse must remain almost motionless. Without a twitch, Clarke's experienced mare lets a thrilled child pat her nose.

Traditionally the sentries in Whitehall are there to secure the approach to Buckingham Palace, but one of their chief duties now is ignoring the tourists.

5

The West End

To people who do not know London very well the West End means elegance, fashion, and the sight of the moneyed classes going about their pleasurable affairs. Once this was true. It is true no longer, but the error is so persistent that I begin by quoting someone who knows the West End better than most, for he has spent his adult life there.

The major theatres of England are in the West End; Harold Hobson is a drama critic for a Sunday paper that is the voice of the Establishment, *The Sunday Times*. That is to say that night after night he sits in the most expensive seats for the most fashionable of occasions, a first night. Someone having written that there are too many dinner jackets and tiaras in such audiences for the good of the theatrical art, Hobson responded that the writer "is living in a romantic fantasy long since passed away. Dinner jackets are as rare as clogs, and in the whole of my experience as a theatre-goer, I have never seen a tiara". He goes on to say that the Paris theatre can still dress fashionably, but it is no longer so in London. "The nearest we get to *haute couture*," Hobson wrote, with a bit of pardonable hyperbole, "is tights by Marks and Spencer", this latter being a chain store famous for its cheap ready-made clothing.

In this respect London today differs from most other great cities. Paris has its *tout Paris*, a select group of expensively-dressed people who attend costly parties, and without whom no fashionable occasion is really in the fashion; but London has no "West Enders". New York has its Social Register; the only thing comparable in London is the list of eligible young men that mothers of unmarried daughters make each year, meanwhile despairing because their daughters ignore them. On first nights at La Scala in Milan, there is such a display of jewels that I half expect masked men with guns to walk on the stage in the middle of the opera, and maybe one day they will; if they did that at Covent Garden however, their booty would scarcely pay for the getaway cars.

It is the same in the streets. In bygone novels the sprigs of the aristocracy, beautifully hatted and shod, stroll nonchalantly down Piccadilly. If they did that today the hurrying *hoi-polloi* would briefly conclude they were on the prowl for homosexual prostitutes, with which the street abounds. *Paparazzi*, the ubiquitous photographers of film stars, still haunt Rome's *Via Veneto*. If the stars wish to be photographed in Bond Street, they will have to go to the coin-in-the-slot machine in the Piccadilly Underground.

The West End, then, is not chic. By day it can be drab. Yet as soon as night falls, it becomes the most exciting city centre in all Europe, perhaps in

Advertising lights spin restlessly round the little winged figure of Eros, poised at the heart of the West End in Piccadilly Circus. The statue is a memorial to the Victorian philanthropist, Lord Shaftesbury, after whom Shaftesbury Avenue, London's main theatre street leading out of the Circus, is named.

the world. It offers something to beguile all tastes, from the most elementary to the most cerebral—from whores, let us say, to the music of the contemporary composer Henze. I suppose New York has as much going on, but the New Yorker, while praising his city to the visitor, is compelled to warn him that it may be risky to go to Times Square at night. The West End is not so paradoxical. You will be quite safe in Piccadilly Circus.

This is the centre of the West End. It is very ugly. It is so ugly that there have been proposals to pull it down—a good idea except that the buildings proposed to replace the present ones are uglier still. The only object of artistic merit in the place is a fountain. It is surmounted by a statue of a boy. Londoners, in their hazy way, call this Eros. They hold the statue in great affection because they think it symbolizes sex. They would like it less if they knew that in fact it represents the Angel of Christian Charity, the fountain being a monument to a Victorian worthy, Lord Shaftesbury, a powerful doer of good works. It does not matter much that Londoners call it by the wrong name because there is no such thing in the heavenly choir as an Angel of Christian Charity. The sculptor, Sir Alfred Gilbert, made the whole thing up. The boy is supposed to be poised on a cascade of water. The water was never turned on; as a result, Sir Alfred retired in a huff to the Continent, where he lived for the rest of his days.

From this Circus the West End extends in all directions, but opinions vary as to its boundaries. It used to end on one side at the Thames, but now it has jumped across the river to the opposite bank. North of the river it may be defined as a place always within a few minutes walk of one of London's parks: Park Lane is one of its most famous roads. In this area

The handsome portico of the Haymarket Theatre, silhouetted by bright lamplight, towers above a crowd of playgoers departing after the evening's performance. Founded in 1720, the theatre testifies to London's long and vigorous dramatic traditions. It was rebuilt with its present façade in 1820-1 by John Nash, and completely refitted inside in 1905.

are places, such as Mayfair, which are known as "good addresses". To the north, the West End finishes abruptly in Soho, the worst address in town.

Let us start at the "Eros" fountain. If the good Lord Shaftesbury has lost out with his monument, his name survives in a road which leads away from it. Shaftesbury Avenue is one of London's best-known places, although I doubt whether Shaftesbury would have approved of its fame. It is the centre of the doings of people whom the Victorians thought lewd and licentious: I mean actors. It contains some of London's best-loved theatres. It is full of theatrical memories; and I should like to give my own.

My very first memory of the London theatre was being taken to the "Lyric" to see a musical version of the life of Schubert. I went with my parents and we had seats under the circle. I spent a part of the time whispering to my father because he sat behind a pillar that obscured his view of what went on in one-third of the stage, so he had to rely on me to tell him. A more recent memory of the theatre is that of going by myself to the "Cambridge" to see a musical version of the life of Jesus Christ. I bought an expensive seat in the stalls—and sat behind a pillar that obscured a little more than one-third of the stage. I needed no-one to whisper to me, because I already knew the plot. The entertainment had a happy ending for me because, from where I was sitting, I could not be sure whether Christ was crucified or not.

The theatre is one of England's ancient glories, and the visitor must make the best he can of her ancient theatres. If he sits behind a pillar at the "Lyric", he can console himself with the thought that from the same seat in 1893 he would not have been able to see Eleanora Duse make her first London appearance. Besides, it is his own fault. The pillar is marked on the box-office plan by a black circle the size of a pin head. If he buys a seat behind it, it is not the duty of the seller to tell him he needs his eyes tested.

There are other hazards, one of which is the attendant who will show you to your seat. In most other countries, you tip this person. In London you do not. She is usually an elderly woman who accepts your ticket with an expression that says you would be far better off on your knees in church. This demeanour spreads to the audience, which seats itself in silence. I have heard more noise from mourners gathering for a funeral in Naples than from a London audience expecting a roaring farce.

Bars are provided for drinking during the intervals; this convenience seems most civilized to a New York theatregoer but it, too, can be disconcerting. The bars are usually so small that they are instantly packed, largely with people who, like you, will be unable to get a drink before the bell rings. The superior people casually consuming whiskies really *are* superior people. They have ordered their drinks before the show began, and have found them waiting for them on little bits of paper with their names on them. There is no quicker way for a foreigner to earn the respect of a Londoner than for him to adopt this little stratagem.

Sight-lines are another hurdle. The Greeks and the Romans built theatres from which every citizen could see the stage over the heads of the citizens in front of him; thus, the playgoer did not have to rock on his rump from side to side. The secret seems to have been lost along with so much of the Greco-Roman dramatic output. Under the benign care of the Welfare State, the stature of the British people is (I am told) increasing. After a few evenings in the London theatre, I believe it.

In fairness it must be said that, very slowly, London is building modern theatres worthy of her great heritage. The world comes to see and hear British actors, and perhaps in the newer theatres they will be able to do both. These performers are supremely good, and we might pause to ask why.

Putting all psychology aside, an actor and an actress must be in complete command of his feet, his legs, his hands, his expression and his voice. Without that, he should stick to the cinema. The historian of the film, Paul Rotha, has recorded that Garbo, in her earlier films, was so jerky in her movements that some sequences were shot in slow motion. That sort of thing does not do for the London stage, however good-looking the performer. Gerald du Maurier, the great master of the British style of acting, once held an audience (including myself) spellbound while, without speaking a word, and in a most leisurely manner, he made up an impromptu bed on a couch, pulled the curtains, loosened his clothes, smoked a cigarette, and quietly went to sleep. Later, in his dressing room, he showed me a little of the vast technique that went into the wordless triumph. Thus, in picking up a glass, he would advance his *wrist* towards it first, until his fingers were in the exact position that the gesture called for.

And so on. But the secret lay deeper than that. Du Maurier customarily portrayed the English gentleman. Now everybody in England is brought up to control his movements and expressions. Merely look around at the audience coming in, or sitting in silence for the curtain to rise, and it will be seen that this is so. All over Europe after the Second World War, the favourite way of boys to mimic an American G.I. was to put their feet up on a table. An Englishman can put his feet on a table only when he has attained the dignity of the Front Benches of the House of Commons. Although his expression is often described as wooden, it must be admitted that it is perfectly under control. His whole upbringing gives him the equipment essential for fine acting.

It is this perfect self-command that the London theatregoer buys his ticket to see. This ticket buyer is the despair of people who speak of the Theatre with a capital "T". He goes indifferently to plays with a message that will save the world, or plays that raise questions no deeper than to ask if there is anyone for tennis. He keeps playwrights in their place, which is to entertain him, and not instruct. The playwright may indeed intend a message; but he will not convey it to the Londoner if he does not also entertain. Nowadays the Londoner has no class prejudices. The play he attends may

Burlington Arcade, constructed between 1815 and 1819, provides a serene precinct for luxury shopping just off noisy, crowded Piccadilly. It was said to have been built by an angry peer, owner of Burlington House, along the edge of his grounds to prevent Bond Street tradesmen tossing litter over his garden wall.

be about the well-heeled and brilliant or those whose conversation takes place at the kitchen sink. He has few of the high expectations that the New Yorker has of his writers, such as Arthur Miller or Tennessee Williams, and as a consequence he does not share their disappointments. At the height of his world fame, Bernard Shaw could not be certain of a run of more than a few weeks for a new play. Those that did succeed owed their longer runs to such accomplished players as Sybil Thorndike or Cedric Hardwicke. When, in his later years, he became all Shaw with no good parts for actors, his plays lay long in his drawer before they were presented. Broadway dimmed its lights when Shaw died; Shaftesbury Avenue made no gesture.

Great performers from foreign lands, acting in a foreign style, are briefly observed for a week or two, and then play to half-empty theatres. In spite of the vast renown of American film stars, no American actor has won any permanent following in the London theatre. Occasionally an American actress will draw an amused audience in a musical play, but it is her unrestrained and undisciplined vigour that pleases, for a while.

Nor can the London theatregoer be led by the nose by critics as the New Yorker and the Parisian can. Bad notices do not automatically damn a London play. I began my writing career as a drama critic in the West End. I was very young and very full of what I conceived to be my power. Older colleagues who sat beside me in the stalls, and whose names I revered, were kind to me. They praised my prose style but gently informed me that nobody took any notice of Press reviews except the performers. Their columns in the Sunday newspapers were read with appreciation, but by people who lived in the provinces and went to the London theatre once a year, if that. I soon gave up the job. Subsequently a brilliant critic, Kenneth Tynan, also young, wrote in exasperation that the West End theatre was dominated by a member of the audience that he christened "Aunt Agatha". Everybody agreed. He, too, left the job.

I have found that in New York, Paris, Berlin, Rome and Milan the play director is either reverenced or condemned. It is "his" production of such-and-such a play that is discussed in the Press, in the clubs and during the intervals of the show. He is much discussed in London, too, but only in strictly professional circles. Tyrone Guthrie was a director of genius, the first to think of doing Shakespeare on trapezes. He emigrated to the western world and did not return. He was followed by Peter Brook, a man of equal inventive power. He, too, emigrated, to Paris. It is instructive to engage a London theatregoer in conversation about his memories. They will be about *Gielgud's* "Hamlet", *Thorndike's* "St. Joan", *Edith Evans'* "Way of the World", or *Olivier's* "The Entertainer". As for scene designers, their names are not known to the paying public at all. England produced a stage designer who changed theatrical history all over the world. The simple, unitary sets we all see were his invention. A theatrical critic (the same Kenneth Tynan) wondered whatever had happened to him. He

Small Shops of Big Repute

Certain long-established shops still convey the feeling of an era when London—the London that counted—was confined to a small central area, and when shopping was a more personal matter between tradesman and patron than it generally is now. The shops themselves are often small, especially those that have been at the same address for many decades, and their interior fittings make a virtue of their lack of modernity.

These examples are: J. Floris the perfume shop, established in 1739 and run today by direct descendants of its founder; Allen's, a family butcher's shop that has plied its trade in Mayfair for two centuries; the cheese shop of Paxton and Whitfield, the best known in London; and the bow windows of Fribourg and Treyer, snuff and tobacco sellers since 1720 and specialists in cigars.

Cheese in Jermyn Street

Perfume in Jermyn Street

Meat in Mount Street

Tobacco in the Haymarket

found the great Gordon Craig in a cheap boarding house in the south of France, lonely, forgotten and, as the critic noticed, in need of a good meal.

In London the actor is all. If I were to find a reason for this, I would put it down to Shakespeare. The London theatregoer has been exposed to him at school. There he finds him incomprehensible without footnotes or a teacher to explain the archaic language. Actors, who are rarely students of literature, also find his language incomprehensible. They will recite the famous passages of poetry in a duly sonorous fashion, but there is a lot in Shakespeare that cannot be made comprehensible. Still, out there is the audience, equally at sea, and it must be entertained. The actors therefore summon all their skills to project a character. Gestures, tricks, expressions, humour or sheer force of theatrical personality are marshalled to get the player over the awkward bits. Then the playgoer finds, as he sits in the dark, that Shakespeare after all is a good playwright, and he is eternally grateful to the man or woman on the stage who brought him the revelation.

This may be too personal an explanation; it is certainly what I have felt. Perhaps we should merely say that the British are the best actors, as we say that Italians are the best singers and Russians the best dancers.

Napoleon had a generalization all of his own about the British. He said that they were a nation of shopkeepers. If they are, then all the best shops in the country are in the West End of London. They have been famous for over a century. One hundred years ago you did not go window-shopping. If you had the money to shop in the best shops, you knew which they were. Quite probably your father had told you; if not, then certainly your fellow Club men. There were shops for your hats, your boots, your shirts, your jewellery and so on. There were shops where your son was sent to buy his school uniform, and shops where you went to buy your own uniforms— those for hunting, or banquets, or tramping the moors in pursuit of small game. You assumed that the articles you bought were the best. Even if they were not, you were not inclined to argue, since you always had an enormous bill owing to the shopkeeper who would not press you unduly to pay. You thought nothing of being in debt, since you had been encouraged to run up bills in your youth, when you studied at the older universities. Sometimes, of course, you never did pay all your bills but that did not matter. The West End had long ago invented the system that has subsequently been so successful elsewhere under the name of hire-purchase: the price was increased to cover interest and loss through defaulters as well, of course, as the prestige of the correct label. The prices asked to this day in such places as Burlington Arcade are something of a historic relic. Nor are they dishonest. A few minutes walk outside the West End and you can often buy the same article one-third cheaper. But you will not have the label to boost your confidence when you are ordering a meal in some smart hotel.

Because the shopkeepers had no need of ostentatious display, the

Astride a wooden horse and reflected in expertly angled mirrors, a client of Huntsman's, the Savile Row tailors, discusses the fit of a sleeve. The wooden horse is kept at hand, complete with saddle, to ensure that the clothes fit well when the owner goes riding.

windows of the shops in the West End do not have the opulent splendour of those in Rome's Via Condotti or New York's Fifth Avenue. In the days of their world hegemony, the shops of the West End did not bother to have plate glass. They stuck to small panels through which you were meant merely to glance. The visitor in search of these shop fronts will find some in Bloomsbury, in a narrow lane called Woburn Walk.

No: you must not expect to window-shop. You must pluck up courage and go inside. And about what you will find there I have some inside information. In one of those vagaries that all young writers go through when they temporarily lose faith in themselves, I ran, for a few months, a publicity organization (if I can use the word "organization" at all) which had its offices in 49, Dover Street, a very fashionable place for shopping. How fashionable it was can be shown by the fact that on the ground floor a Russian Prince called Yousoupoff had a shop where he sold perfumes at extravagant prices, although he really preferred to tell his distinguished customers how he had helped to shoot Rasputin. All the perfumes of Arabia could not wash *that* stain from his hand; and unlike Lady Macbeth, he did not want them to, because it was very good for business.

He and the shopkeepers of similarly elegant places in the street would foregather at local cocktail bars and restaurants, and among their company I gathered much about the way they worked over a customer. Their regular customers they of course knew. These customers presented no problems because, my neighbours assured me, after early middle-age a regular always bought the same thing or something like it, even when he entered the shop with the firm determination to be up-to-date and move with the times. As for the unknown buyer, they never judged him or her by the clothes. The most impossibly dressed customer was treated as an equal of a peer; it flattered the client and, in any case, he probably was a peer. These shop-keepers judged people by their faces: they could tell if someone had been used to three square meals a day from childhood on. Reception clerks at hotels all over the world have told me that they go by the same rule.

Contrary to what is believed, these shopkeepers do not aim at guiding the customer's taste. The preliminary chit-chat is based on the techniques of palmists and crystal-gazers. It is designed to make the subject reveal himself. Having been shown several items that are quite unsuitable, the very thing he has been looking for is then diffidently produced. The shop-keepers take an artistic pride in having that exact thing, however unsaleable it would be in more plebeian establishments. The manager of a renowned firm of gunsmiths once showed me a double-barrelled gun subtly designed for the sportsman who squinted every time he took aim.

It is a pity to have to record that such well-run shops are one by one disappearing. Famous names vanish from the shop fronts overnight. Their proprietors cannot afford to let the sons of customers run up bills like those their fathers were proud to owe. Tailors can no longer be sure that the

At James Lock and Co., bowler hats stand row on row, their sizes indicated by little white labels. The dome-shaped bowler was designed by an early-19th-Century Earl of Leicester for his game-beaters—it was knocked off by branches less readily than the top hats then worn—and spread to the upper classes, becoming in time an almost essential part of the attire of a City businessman.

well-off world will come to Savile Row for its suits. Their clients may well go to Rome, where they will be made to look younger at the price of being more uncomfortable. Expert cutters emigrate to New York or Buenos Aires, where they can make much more money. Saddlers, adept in perfectly fitting distinguished bottoms, are being driven to the wall by the enormous appetite horses have for their ever more expensive foodstuffs. Hatters wonder if their product will go the way of the peruke. Boot-and-shoe makers have more hope. A hand-made shoe under the directors' table is still a mark of success. But they come much cheaper in Hong Kong. And so the genteel shops are being more and more replaced by tawdry boutiques, huge department stores and, to all appearances, more shoe stores than there are in any other city in the world.

One sort of West End shop is, however, making a great deal of money. Its representatives are among the West End's most satisfying pleasures, and it is surprising how few people enjoy them. It might be imagined that a well-warmed, thick-carpeted, excellently lit shop where you will never be asked to buy anything would be crowded. They are not. They are the art galleries of Bond Street, Bruton Street, St. James's Square, Cork Street, Albemarle Street and a few other favoured spots. Their business is to sell pictures, and since the value of paper money in all its forms has declined, they do sell pictures in very satisfactory quantities. How they do it is, at first, something of a mystery, for their proprietors appear to make no effort. They display their wares, or some of them, tastefully. They advertise in newspapers. That is all. Their doors are open to anyone who has the courage to push them open, and no matter how deeply or how long you study an exhibit, you will never be pressed to buy. Here again, it does not matter in the least how you are dressed. The bearded man in sandals and a dirty old shirt may be some painter whose verdict is law among the connoisseurs. The woman who is made up like a tart may be the current mistress of some great artist whose works sell like hot cakes. Whoever you are, you are left completely in peace.

Unless you wish otherwise. Introducing a university student to this London delight, I took him to one of the grandest and oldest galleries, Agnew's. He asked a question of one of the attendants. It was about a Rubens sketch, selling at a vast price. Some minutes later I found him sitting on the floor with the same attendant, priceless sketches of Rubens' contemporaries around him, listening to an expert lecture. Months later, in the same gallery, I asked one of the principals why they had taken so much trouble over an obviously inpecunious young man. He said: "He took the trouble to ask a question. And we here act on a piece of advice my grandfather once gave me. 'Never,' he said 'ignore a young girl: you never know whom she will marry.' It's the same with us. You would be surprised at the sort of people who actually, when at last they can afford it, collect pictures. And *I* am continuously surprised at the people who don't."

About these latter, he had an anecdote. The famous picture dealer Duveen had acquired a magnificent collection of old masters. Of the handful of people who could afford to buy it, Duveen picked as his target Henry Ford, the man of the Tin Lizzie. Ford proving unapproachable through the usual channels, Duveen had the collection photographed in full colour, and printed in a large volume. This book he sent to Ford. The great man replied in a personal letter. "My wife and I", he wrote, "greatly enjoyed your beautiful book. The paintings are so well reproduced that we do not feel it is necessary for us to buy them."

The gallery owner thus must have an open mind. Let us suppose that you have a sum of money—a legacy, perhaps—that you feel could buy you a worthwhile picture. You visit a West End gallery. One picture on the walls takes your fancy. You ask the price. It is far beyond the sum you meant to spend. You say so. Perhaps you feel embarrassed. You need not be. You will be politely asked what amount you had in mind. You confess it. You will be given a chair, or taken to a back room, and from then on you will pass an hour of enchantment, as picture after picture is brought up from the basement. It is there that the gallery keeps its real store. Among the pictures that will suit your purse, you will also be shown one or two old masters of incalculable value, just as a compliment. You will leave the gallery, minus your legacy, but the possessor of a painting, or even a drawing, by some great name, that has taken your heart entirely.

The Londoners I have so far described, with a few exceptions, have all been very English—City merchants, Heralds, dukes, earls and cultivated shopkeepers. But anyone "coming up" to the West End (as the phrase goes) will pay a visit to a part of London that is English only in the taxes its inhabitants pay (if they positively have to). This is Soho, and it has been full of foreigners for centuries. Even the name sounds foreign to British ears, although it is derived from a cry which huntsmen used to call off their hounds when the area now termed Soho was still countryside. When in the 17th Century the Huguenots fled from France because of Catholic persecution, they settled here. Frenchmen fleeing yet another persecution, that of the Revolution, followed them to the same place. The French were very grateful for British asylum, but they could not carry gratitude to the point of eating British cooking. Foreign food, foreign menus and foreign odours became the marks of Soho, and they still are.

Until the middle of this century, every good Britisher knew that as well as having perverted palates, foreigners were inclined to have unhealthy minds, particularly about sex. The Victorians and the Edwardians thought that this was all right in its place, which was across the English Channel, or in that warren of streets leading nor'-nor'-west from Shaftesbury Avenue where foreigners congregated; namely, Soho. Here the British, in a furtive and ashamed way, would go hunting flesh, but no longer in the shape of foxes. Two culinary adjectives were used by Londoners to describe Soho:

for some it was "spicy", to others it was "unsavoury", and neither word had anything to do with the cooking.

Then, as the middle of the 20th Century passed, the permissive society came into being. Soho flourished. From being the haunt of petty crooks and hard-working street walkers, Soho blossomed out into striptease and nude shows, cinemas for blue films and tastefully furnished apartments for call girls. For red-blooded men, or those who wished to be thought so, a visit to the West End has come to include an obligatory visit to Soho.

The foreign eating houses flourished as well. English people began to travel abroad in great numbers. Some of them returned with a certain sense of shame at finding that the English as a nation were held to subsist largely on fish and chips. This minority went to Soho to lunch and dine when they wished to celebrate, and there were enough of this elite to cram Soho's eating houses to the doors. Italians and Greeks and Indians had followed the French. Restaurants of box-like dimensions, which had been set up to feed economy-minded foreigners and students, found their names bandied about in high circles. The proprietors raised their prices accordingly; and it is now both fashionable and expensive to have one's own favourite Soho restaurant, with a personal welcome from the owner.

Because of this, Soho has remained a quiet place to visit in the evening. It has avoided the honky-tonk atmosphere that threatens to ruin such places as *le vieux carré* in New Orleans. Soho's two worlds are kept apart. You may eat dinner without being solicited, or make love without smelling of garlic, according to your choice. The advertisements of the strip shows and cinemas are unobtrusive. They can even be high-toned. I have noted one that proclaims its wares with blown-up photographs, all quite proper, from "Le Baiser" by Rodin, a bas-relief from the Hindu temple at Khajurao, and a detail from a picture by Renoir.

All great cities have their red-light districts, but few are as cautious and respectable as London's. In Soho the light is not so much red as amber. Perhaps it is due to history. The Huguenots were intensely respectable Frenchmen, which is one of the reasons why they were sent packing. At midnight, in Soho's empty and sparsely-lit streets, the visitor might well feel that their spirits still walk.

The Londoner and His Parks

A sudden flurry of April sleet whips past a woman and her sheepdog walking along Hyde Park's Serpentine, where a week before people were sunbathing.

Londoners use their royal parks, once the private pleasure grounds of kings, as a back garden where they can pursue their diverse activities, in their own often solitary ways. While a sunny day may temporarily cram the parks with lunchtime sun-seekers, it is at more unlikely times—a wet afternoon (above), a soft evening, or early in the morning—that the intimate side of a Londoner's relationship with his parks is subtly revealed.

Both Hyde Park and Regent's Park lie within a 15-minute stroll from Oxford Circus. In the heart of either it is possible to be far out of sight and smell of traffic, oblivious of the city and even of other people, surrounded only by lawns, flowers or tall trees where a startling variety of wild birds nest and breed. Here, Londoners come in ones and twos to breathe the fresh air, collect their thoughts and be themselves.

With the judicious air of a teacher addressing her class, a woman dispenses bread to an attentive group of Canada geese at the lake in St. James's Park.

His head down against the dazzle of early morning sun that gilds the budding trees, a runner passes an unperturbed pair of wild grey herons in Regent's Park.

A regular user of Kensington Gardens has selected a sheltered spot for the day. Her equipment includes sunglasses, overcoat, knitting, and bread for the birds.

Into the chilly lake goes one of the spartan all-the-year-round swimmers in Hyde Park. The spring sun lights but does not warm his winter-pale limbs.

On the deserted shore of the Serpentine, an umbrella draped with polythene protects two anglers and a child from the chill of a grey winter afternoon.

A regimental band framed by a graceful canopied bandstand, gives a concert to empty deck-chairs in Hyde Park. Bands play in the big parks in summer.

A single seagull floats over the glittering water of the Serpentine, where a hired boat, its striped sail filled by the evening breeze, tacks along the lake.

An autumn evening sky and the rich foliage of majestic plane trees envelop a neatly turned-out girl riding along a bridlepath in Hyde Park.

6

Clubland and a Revolution

"Disestablishmentarianism": that was the smart reply when I was a school-boy and another boy asked: "Bet you don't know the longest word in the English language!" We said it very slowly: "Dis-es-tablish-ment-arian-ism", and none of us, if I remember, knew what it meant. Later I learned that it was the name of a movement to remove the Anglican church from the rule of the monarch. Much later still I found it could describe one of the deepest revolutions that London has ever undergone, and which had nothing to do with religion whatsoever.

In the heart of the word is "establishment". The heart of the English Establishment is in the West End of London; it is there I wish to begin. Running from Haymarket towards the palace of St. James's is a handsome street known as Pall Mall. It is exclusive: so exclusive that the ordinary man-in-the-other-streets never knows how it should be pronounced and is shy about trying it. Most of his acquaintances will make both words rhyme with "shall" (in the U.S. they may pronounce it "Pell Mell"). But if you are invited to visit one of the residents in the institutions that line the street, you will probably be asked to "Pawl Mawl". If you lose your way and ask a passer-by to direct you to "Pawl Mawl", you will be told, but your informant will think you are putting on the dog. Anyone who considers this paragraph the height of triviality does not yet know London.

The mystery must be unveiled slowly, step by step. Pall Mall is lined with Clubs (to any Londoner, his club deserves a capital "C"). All the Pall Mall Clubs are famous, and still other famous Clubs are clustered close at hand. The idea is that the Clubs must be close to each other; the distance might be defined as that which a Club Member might walk under an umbrella in a shower of rain without getting wet. If the shower is heavy, he can hail a taxi from the steps of one Club, and the driver will willingly take him to the other Club. If an ordinary person were to ask a taxi-driver to take him so short a distance anywhere else in London, the driver would tell him where he could take himself, and the destination would not be a Club.

London Clubs are mostly old. Some date from the period when the first Georgian squares were being built. White's, for instance, was founded in 1693. Mr. White was a companionable man who served hot chocolate in his shop and did well. Soon the shop became the centre of London's wildest gambling. New premises, much grander, were built, and the great of the land foregathered there. Another gambling Club followed, called Brooks's. Charles James Fox, statesman and inveterate gambler, was once observed there on the day that he had lost his whole fortune. He was reading Horace.

Serene silence reigns between the book-lined walls of the South Library of the Athenaeum, which is by reputation the most intellectual of the London Clubs. Among the literary lights who have worked in this tall, quiet first-floor room are W. M. Thackeray, Lord Macaulay, Matthew Arnold and Charles Dickens.

Asked why he was reading Horace at such a time, he replied, "Why, what else should I be doing?" Thus he set the tone for the proper behaviour of a Club Member in adversity, from that day to this.

For instance, yet another Club, almost as old, is Boodle's. Mr. Boodle is quite unknown to history, but his name is now mentioned with awe, because Boodle's is a very exclusive Club indeed. In 1974, an ex-Prime Minister was dining there when he was informed that somebody had thrown a bomb inside his private residence. He was not reading Horace but he preserved a Roman calm. Asked for his opinion of the event, he sagely observed that had he been in the room, he would have been hit. The laws of Newton having been vindicated, Mr. Edward Heath had no further comment. Again, the perfect Club Member.

There is, by the way, no such thing as a "club*man*". This is a vulgarism used only by people who do not belong to the best Clubs. A Club Member is by definition a man. Women are not elected. Until these degenerate times, they were not even allowed to set foot in a Club. A Club Member can stay at the Club for one or several nights. Should he have a quarrel with his wife, he does not make up his bed on the sofa. He retires to his Club, which then becomes a harem in reverse, since it is inviolate by the female sex.

London Clubs are exclusive, but they are not aristocratic. There is a Club for every sort of gentleman, provided he can be trusted to behave like one. The Athenaeum, for instance, rather aims at bishops, and the sort of people who can get on with bishops. The Savage is quite different. It is meant for writers. Mr. Richard Savage was one, a journalist. In 1743 he died of starvation in Covent Garden Market, then the centre of London's trade in fruit and vegetables. Other writers, struck by the contrast of one of their profession dying of want in the middle of plenty, founded the Club in his name. The Club still exists; it is still primarily for writers. Few of its members would nowadays die of want, but of course it is still possible. If one did succumb to starvation, he would undoubtedly have the decency to resign from the Savage first.

Exclusive societies of males have been known throughout history, but they have all been distinguished by the fact that the members gather together for the purpose of doing something. The secret societies of primitive Africa practise magic; Dominican monks pursue learning; Masons help one another; the Jesuits defend the Papacy. The great London Clubs are, by contrast, male gatherings dedicated to doing nothing at all. Of course, for a human being to do absolutely nothing needs the highly specialized skills that yogis develop in the Himalayas. These are not to be found in the Clubs, but a Member who merely sits in the same chair in the same window in all but complete silence, and leaves it only to eat and answer the calls of nature, is much admired, and is pointed out with pride to new Members. This firm belief in the *dolce far niente* is an essential in Club life, and it must be firmly grasped for that life to be understood. I have been

On the menu at one of London's best-known restaurants is this tribute to the glory of British beef: to import the staple of a Simpson's meal would be an abomination. The cartoon is one of a successful series, drawn in the 1920s by H. M. Bateman, pinpointing with devastating iconoclasm some of the beliefs of the British about themselves and their values.

entertained in foreign imitations, and the difference is fatal. In the Racquet Club of New York, the furnishings are the same as in London—the comfortable leather chairs, the dull pictures on the walls and the discreet servants who appear to move on soundless castors. But there is a distressing air of activity in the members, a sense that once off the leash they will bolt through the door and get back to their desks. There is even a feeling that they might actually play racquets, and be keen on the game. In London this would never do. Not even good conversation is encouraged, and brilliant talk is deplored. Dr. Samuel Johnson had a sort of club of his own, which included such dazzling talkers as Garrick, Gibbon and the Doctor himself. In a true London Club, Johnson would have been blackballed as a bore.

The word "blackball" has passed into the English language as a synonym for silent disapproval for which no explanation is required or given. It comes from a ritual that might have been invented by Franz Kafka. The Club is governed by a committee of Members. A new Member is proposed and seconded before this committee, which then votes by slipping, with due concealment, a ball into a bag. The balls are black for "no", white for "yes", and a single black ball signifies rejection. In this way a Member may turn down his own blood-brother without anybody being the wiser.

How are candidates selected? To have attained eminence in your walk of life is not enough. Generally speaking, merit, both inside and outside the Club, counts for little in estimating a man. Aneurin Bevan was considered one of the most brilliant politicians of his age. A socialist, he was at one time eyed as an almost certain Prime Minister. Visiting a London Club as a guest, he was kicked down the steps by a Member who did not like his views. The incident was widely discussed in the Clubs. It was agreed that the site of the kicking was correct: Aneurin's bottom, and the steps. The motive was considered adequate: Aneurin's views were anathema to members of that particular Club, so he should not have gone there. The matter was finally decided with much finesse. Since Bevan was a member of His Majesty's Privy Council and a Minister of the Crown, the deed could be construed as showing a lack of respect for the monarchy. The kicker made a very limited apology, and resigned from the Club.

To be fit for one of the great London Clubs, one must be *nurtured*. This process is so much a part of London life, I must describe it. I do so willingly, for it has great charm.

Well-bred Englishmen have a horror of showing any affection for their sons after they have left the nursery. They are handed over to schoolmasters in "public" (i.e. private) schools. Discipline is strict, but it is not aimed to give a boy polish. He can leave school as much a lout as a soldier.

It is left to his family to teach him how to behave in the society of his equals. The first stage in this instruction takes place when the boy is on holiday. At the age of, say, 14, he is taken out to luncheon. This may be done by his father or, more frequently, an uncle. The restaurant chosen is a grand one. Traditionally, it is Simpson's, in the Strand. Simpson's is large. The ground floor is reserved for male customers, and it is staffed with elderly and experienced waiters.

The boy is naturally shy and awkward. But from the moment he sees the head waiter to the time he leaves the restaurant, everything miraculously goes all right. He, not his host, is the centre of attention. With the most subtle of gestures he is guided round the pitfalls of knives, forks, spoons, napkins and glasses. When the carver wheels in the beef for which the restaurant is world-famous, he mysteriously finds himself ordering the best cut, which is deferentially served him. Wines inappropriate to the course are deftly removed if he has not drunk them; he is guided away from too ostentatious sweets; and, he does not know how, for the first time in his life he finds himself choosing a liqueur. He tips the doorman who calls the taxi, his uncle having muttered advice in the foyer, and he watches the man salute him in a golden dream.

Two or three ritual meals of this sort, spaced at annual intervals, and he is ready for his first visit to the Club.

Let us suppose that his uncle is a member of the Athenaeum. The boy, or stripling as he now is, is invited to luncheon. The Athenaeum can be described as formal, stuffy, or a mortuary, according to one's mood. For a lad it is, in prospect, terrifying. He knows that in a Club there are certain things one can do, and others one must never do. He has never been told what specifically those things might be. Vaguely he might know that one does not offer to buy a Member a drink. But does one laugh heartily, a man among men, or chuckle, a man among bishops? Does one walk in boldly, as at home, or does one wait at the door, as at a headmaster's study? He mounts the Athenaeum's broad steps as he would those of a church of an unfamiliar faith. Before he enters, he might give a sad glance up the road to Piccadilly Circus, a rumble in the distance from the land of the living.

A porter fixes him with a cold stare from within a glass box. The lad clears his throat. He mutters his uncle's name. Instantly, the porter bursts into a broad welcoming grin. "You must be so-and-so", he says. "You're expected." He emerges from his box, and directs the boy through more portals to where he will find his uncle waiting for him. The boy has been treated as a grown-up. He enters the Club head-high and firm of step. He is not to know that all this has been arranged beforehand—not, that is, until years later he asks the hall-porter to give a welcome to a nephew of his own.

He meets his uncle; his uncle's friends meet him. What strikes him is that this is not like home, where he is always a child, or school, where he is always a boy. Here he is treated as though he is already a Member. There are no curious glances from the men reading newspapers in armchairs. When other Members speak to him, it is without that mawkish kindliness that middleaged men put on to show that they were once a boy too, and that it was The Best Time of Their Lives.

Cricket is still a popular sport at many London schools, including Westminster, whose players are shown turned out in their whites for a spirited game. Half a mile from the school's historic buildings in the shadow of Westminster Abbey, the playing fields and pavilion occupy the centre of spacious Vincent Square, which takes its name from a former headmaster and Dean of Westminster who in 1810 enclosed ten acres of then open land as a sportsground.

He is taken to luncheon. He knows how to behave; Simpson's, or a similar place, has seen to that. Now he must learn to talk. His uncle speaks of their relatives, and the lad is astonished at the almost scandalous freedom with which he does so. While Cousin Arthur's notorious but hushed-up peculiarities are being paraded in a loud voice, the boy peeks anxiously over his shoulder at the other Members. They appear to be deaf. Uncle and nephew retire to another room, and, sunk deeply in a leather armchair, the boy too waxes bold over his coffee and brandy. Three p.m. finds him strolling along Pall Mall, every inch a member of the Establishment, if anyone can be said to be established who is walking on air.

As his tastes develop, he will be taken to other Clubs. There he will see celebrities—actors with knighthoods, for instance—behaving like ordinary human beings, which they certainly do not elsewhere. Should he have literary ambitions, he will meet famous writers who will give him sage advice, such as, "Nothing, my friend, is certain with the Americans until you see the bill" (Hugh Walpole to the present writer.) Or perhaps in some Tory stronghold during a political crisis he will hear the sort of inside talk that one finds in novels by Trollope or Disraeli.

But it was Disraeli who said that England was made up of two nations, the privileged and the poor. I shall record how the underdog had his day, and how disestablishmentarianism shook the Clubs to their foundations.

Not even the closest observer can be absolutely sure how and where it all began. England emerged from the Second World War with the conviction that, all in all, nothing much had happened. London was badly battered; but there was nothing wrong that bricks, mortar and ferro-concrete could not put right. A lot of money had been lost; British enterprise would soon make up the deficiency. The casualties had been far less than had been feared; there had been no massacre of the promising young men, as had happened in Flanders. Many of the promising young men had found safe jobs in a technological war. The social classes were much as before. The upper classes made wise concessions to the less well-off. Hypochondria, the permanent malaise of the British, had been dealt with by a generous free health service, set up by that same man whose kicking down the steps of a Club I have described.

The London theatre, in particular, went on much as before. But in a peripheral theatre, away from Shaftesbury Avenue, a company financed by a dilettante American began to produce the most peculiar plays. One of these, a drama called "Look Back in Anger", was by an unknown writer, John Osborne. The leading character was not looking back at anything, but he was extremely angry at what he saw in front of his eyes. This was a world entirely run by precisely the sort of people we have been examining in their Clubs—an elite, a cabal, a mutual back-scratching clique, an Establishment. The central figure's principal hatred was the Sunday newspapers, where the Establishment expressed its views with the self-certainty of Moses

Silently drinking his regular evening pint of stout, a dark-suited, cloth-capped Londoner takes his repose in the peace of his local pub in Fulham Road. For him the pub serves much the same function as a club does for a rich man.

coming down from Sinai. Jimmy Porter, the character in question, disagreed with those views with a remarkable flow of vulgar invective. He had nothing to put in place of the Establishment, which was perhaps why he had such an appeal to the audience; as I have said, the West Ender reacts favourably only to what entertains him. Jimmy Porter was not grinding an axe; he was swinging it wildly around his head. Jimmy Porter came from the lower classes. The voice of these people had been heard in the theatre before. There had been such plays as "Love on the Dole" and "The Silver Box". These asked for pity. Jimmy asked no one's pity. He was confident that he was right and They—the Establishment—were wrong.

The success of "Look Back in Anger" produced a wave of imitators in the field of the drama, the novel, journalism and above all in the jokesters who hammer out scripts for radio and television comedians. Meanwhile, somewhat ironically, Osborne and the earlier of his imitators passed rapidly into the Establishment itself; like the Club Members, they freely gave of their opinions that the country was going to the dogs. The Establishment, having surrounded, captured, and digested the rebels like an amoeba, rested content.

But only for a while. The Establishment could go to the theatre and watch with a tolerant smile the rantings of various Jimmy Porters, and chuckle at the sight of a kitchen sink on the stage and the noise of a flushed toilet in the wings. They were quite unaware that they faced ruin at the hands of some brash young English lads and a clever young woman.

The English upper crust had always attached great importance to trivialities, particularly when they concerned the appearance of the male sex. The width of a lapel, the number of buttons on a waistcoat, the design of a sock and the length of one's hair were all governed by rules that the young man had to obey or be cast into outer darkness beyond the Club's doors. An effeminate attention to the minutiae of dress had characterized the English upper classes since the days of Beau Brummell. It was now carried to an extreme. I can recall the mysterious law that dictated that one should leave the *last* button of a waistcoat always undone. We have seen something like this in the evolution of the bowler and folded umbrella, which I have mentioned. I am told (and I am quite content to leave it as hearsay) that this custom of the unbuttoned button arose in the adolescent passion for secret signs in Eton (or maybe Harrow). Another secret sign was that one should never wear button-cuffs on one's shirt-sleeves, but—instead, cufflinks. Hair had to be worn short in a peculiarly ugly manner designed, it would appear, to keep incompetent barbers in employment. This last was a key matter. I recall an advertisement from the English tourist authorities, published in an American magazine in the Fifties. It detailed some British attractions, and wound up, "You will, maybe, get a British Haircut. And why not? It is good for you."

On a more serious level, there was a shortage of labour in Britain. The older generation, tired out with the strain and excitements of the war, were unwilling to work. Young people were much in demand and were paid handsomely. Lads, being lads, spent their money on clothes. The suits in the shops being unbearably dull, some tailors revived the Edwardian style, a more flamboyant fashion, long dead. The lads who wore it were called "Teddy Boys", Teddy being an affectionate diminutive for Edward. Very soon the diminutive had lost all affectionate overtones, for the boys, elegantly attired, let all hell loose on the streets. Rival gangs, even more fantastically attired, fought them. The gangs had, of course, their girl companions. These were known as "chicks" or "birds", but the gorgeous plumage was all for the boys.

It was at this point that the talented young woman I mentioned earlier saw her opportunity. Mary Quant is a name that has its permanent place in the story of London alongside the other illustrious ones I have mentioned in this chapter. Already the London Museum collects her memorabilia, and has published, under the *imprimatur* of Her Majesty's Stationery Office, a scholarly monograph about her. By taking a pair of scissors and cutting off girls' skirts to a line well above the lower level of Edwardian drawers, she made the chicks and birds as startling as the boys. She went on to produce frocks of the most extravagant design—extravagant, be it noted, only in artistic inspiration, not, as with the Establishment, in expense. The boys, outshone, responded by dressing in every sort of uniform, from that of cowboys to Victorian soldiers. They also grew their hair longer. Foreign tourists began to flock to see the phenomenon, and articles appeared in foreign journals warning intending tourists that if they should see their car being replenished by a pump attendant with hair down to his shoulders, they would assume that he was effeminate at the risk of a punch on the jaw.

Orthodox London surrendered, from Pall Mall to the periphery. It did so willingly. That may seem surprising, but it should not be. The English had become reconciled to the fact that, compared to Italians or Orientals, they were not a good-looking race. They were proud of the complexion of their women, described as being of milk and roses. But to a cynical observer, milk and roses can be reminiscent of a baby's spanked bottom. The bizarre make-up recommended by the daring Mary Quant—pale mask-like faces and garish purplish lipstick—seemed much preferable. As for the young men, they were dressing only in the dashing manner that had been common in London streets right down to the Industrial Revolution. The long, curling hair falling to the shoulders recalled the Restoration. Besides, it was dignified. Did not High Court judges and the Speaker of the House of Commons wear full-bottomed wigs? To many of the older generation the streets of London began to look like a fancy-dress ball. But it had to be admitted that the guests were a handsome-looking lot.

It was a revolution. These London styles swept the rest of the world. Foreign newspapers were filled with reports about it. Unfortunately the writers did not always understand London. They assumed that this freedom of dress implied a freedom of sexual morals. The legend of a "swinging" London arose, to the embarrassment of Londoners, for the truth was that morals in the ancient city that had seen so many wars were no freer than they usually are after an armed conflict. It had been so in the Twenties; it was so again in the Sixties. The Londoner knew it meant nothing very much and soon would pass, as it has done.

But Pall Mall was never the same. It no longer mattered whether you had buttons on your shirt cuffs or whether one was undone on your waistcoat. Bishops, it is true, did not wear their hair down to their dog-collars, but new Members were not blackballed because they were not barbered short back and sides. By the Seventies the Clubs feared for their very existence, although most have managed to survive. The young of the Establishment are still brought up by uncles in the way they should behave. But Club Members no longer regard themselves with the solemn satisfaction of the past. And it is not likely that anybody will ever be kicked down the steps of a Club again.

7

The Cockney: A Farewell

London: January: a year in the middle Seventies. It is five o'clock in the evening. It is dark. Although it is winter, it is only cold enough to make me content that I am on my way to warmth and light and whisky with an old London friend. I am in the Mall, the processional way that rolls from Buckingham Palace to Trafalgar Square. On the opposite side of the road one of John Nash's terraces rises, solemn, ordered and secure, its stuccoed columns amber in the lamplight. I prepare to cross the road. I look left and right and left again. There is no wheeled traffic, but I pause. Three mounted guardsmen trot past me in the gloom. They have huge horses and they wear shining breastplates. Over their shoulders, draped as though on a monument, lie three cloaks, two dark blue, one a brilliant red. There is a jingle of metal, and they are gone.

I cross the road. I am swallowed up in the darkling courtyard of a Tudor palace: St. James's, once the home of the monarchy. But now I walk, unimpeded, between its walls. I pass a sentry in his box, turn right and walk down Pall Mall. I come to a Club; the porter greets me. My friend greets me in the vast hall and we go up in a shuddering, ancient lift to his rooms. They are panelled in white wood. The leather and gold of old books gleams in the lamplight. A Victorian nude by Etty is reflected in a crystal mirror. I am offered some whisky. *Some*, not "a" whisky. Was not the young Somerset Maugham taught that to ask for "a" whisky was a vulgarism smacking of that dreadful American innovation called "a bar"?

We talk of old times. I mention that I have been writing about the monarchy, and he has a tale to tell: how he, a medical specialist of distinction, was asked to join the entourage of the ailing King George VI on some Empire tour, and how George, relaxed beside a fireplace, had advised him to take along a pair of comfortable boots "with good, thick soles, because there's a damned lot of standing about to do in this job".

We go down to dine. The room is enormous, with a high ceiling and great round tables set spaciously apart. I examine the decoration. My host asks me if I can guess when it was built. All that lavishment of gilt? All that abundance of ornament? All that carelessness for expense? Why, then, it must be 1905. "Within a year or two", he agrees. Later, we stroll around the swimming pool. It is big, like everything else. Pillars, massive as those in the baths of the Caesars, hold up a roof lost in darkness. My host says something, but I scarcely hear, I am so taken by the grandeur. Outside, the rain has stopped, so I go for a walk. A few paces and I hear a voice.

"G'd evenin', guv'nor. Can yer spare me the price of a meal?"

Their formality tinged with melancholy recognition of changing times, a local East End Pearly King and Queen stand before a mirror at home. Their button-covered regalia reflects a flamboyant fashion of the late 19th Century when the Pearlies originated, embodying the Cockney community's vigorous affirmation of identity over the then great poverty.

I put my hand in my pocket, but then I pause. "Guv'nor"? Does anybody say that nowadays? And the accent: is it really Cockney? I look closely at the man. He is quite well-dressed; he is clearly well-fed. There is an amused look in his eye.

I ask him, "Where are you from? London?"

"Born within the sound of Bow Bells, guv'nor."

"Rubbish." No Cockney could ever manage that "th" in within; the Cockney pronunciation is "wivin". Besides, there would be at least two diphthongs in Bow. I suspect he thinks I am a tourist.

He replies with dignity, and in the accents of the lower-middle class situation comedies that are the staple of British television.

"Have it your own way," he says, "but I could do with the price of a meal."

I give him a coin, but I have forgotten the rising standard of living. He looks at it and at me. It is clearly not enough for a meal, but he pockets it, nods, and gives me a Maoist stare of disapproval. As he goes without a "goodnight", I remember what my host had said in the Roman bath: "We shall never build anything like that again."

I walked on, knowing that this was the lesson that I, a Londoner, was unwilling to learn. As the 20th Century passed its meridian, London changed, and the Londoner changed with it. It was more than the plumage of Carnaby Street, although that was part of the transformation. The Londoner himself, for centuries so confident, so set in his ways, was becoming a different person. He did not know where he was going any more. All he knew was that he could not go back.

I crossed Trafalgar Square, turned up St. Martin's Lane, and found myself outside a pub called "The Salisbury". This pub had been preserved through all the changes, either by accident, or by the urging of some astute interior designer for the brewers. Etched glass, clearly original, obscured the windows. Inside, bronze figures of buxom women presided over red-plush couches. I sat down and remembered the Cockneys of my youth. They were once as typical of London as those three guardsmen in their cloaks and breastplates. The guardsmen remain, for the tourists. The Cockneys are fading away, and soon nothing will remain of them but their humour, like the grin on the face of Alice's Cheshire Cat. But their humour is as essential a part of London as Big Ben. So we must go in search of the Cockney, even if it means going back into the past.

The word Cockney, say the pundits, originally meant an odd or misshapen egg. It was probably a pejorative applied to the born Londoner by provincial visitors whom the Londoner had taken for a ride. Certainly one Samuel Rowlands, something of a doctor to judge by his surviving writings, said, "I scorn to let a Bow-bell Cockney put me down", so Cockney perkiness existed as far back as 1600, before the Great Fire. By Victorian times the Cockney had spread far beyond the sound of the bells of St. Mary-le-

As if advancing out of a vanishing world a rag and bone man drives his horse forward along a brick alley in the East End. A cement mixer among the rubble alongside him foreshadows the approaching fate of the entire district as it undergoes a wholesale renewal.

Bow, and he had developed a dialect of his own. Dickens thought it consisted of fractured grammar, dropped "h's", and an inability to roll "r's". But the true Cockney was a much more complicated person than Dickens' amiable and subservient Sam Weller.

To hear Cockney we must cross the Thames to a part of London that we have not visited. We first cross London Bridge. Readers with an Anglo-Saxon education in any part of the world will probably have sung a little ditty that goes, "London Bridge is falling down". The London Bridge they have in mind never did fall down. Its fate was full of wry Cockney humour: in modern times it was bought by an American who transported it, stone by stone, to the United States, convinced he had bought Tower Bridge; it was re-assembled, for no one knows what reason, in Lake Havasu City, Arizona. Even so, the American had not bought the London Bridge he had imagined. That was a 12th Century structure lined with houses. After the dwellings were torn down, alcoves were provided along the length of the bridge so that pedestrians could seek refuge from the press of traffic crossing its narrow road. It was replaced in 1831 by the bridge that went to America; and *that* one in turn gave way to the new bridge in 1973. When I cross the new bridge today, I like to think of Shakespeare, on his way to the Globe Theatre, and Chaucer, for at the far end of the bridge his pilgrims set out for Canterbury. Not far from here is the George Inn with balconies from which spectators watched plays in the courtyard. And near by is Southwark Cathedral, sunk several feet deep below London's present level.

I mention all this to prove that, although we have crossed the river, we are still very much in old London. It does not look like it, which is why so few visitors go there. It is a new industrial slum, cleaned up after the bombing but not much improved. It is so ugly that Londoners are ashamed of it.

At the principal crossroads of the area, town councillors have tried to give it a touch of culture. They have erected what must be one of the biggest modern sculptures in the world. It is a metal box full of dents and it is the size of a row of two-storeyed houses. It is irresistibly comic; I expect that future archaeologists, coming upon its remains, will think it is a monument to one of the 20th Century's most famous men—Charlie Chaplin. Sir Charles was born not so far away. And Charlie was a Cockney. The background he brought to his little tramp was Cockney, because the Old Kent Road was the heart of Cockneyland. Here were the barrow-boys and the costermongers, the territory of the Pearly Kings and the Pearly Queens.

The Cockney culture was so compact that it could have made a neat study for an anthropologist. The streets were villages where vast families, pullulating as those in Naples, lived cheek by jowl and in one another's houses. Here is how a pure Cockney, the artist John Allin, describes it. He is speaking of Whitechapel, north of the river; it too is Cockneyland, if somewhat diluted by foreigners, and it will serve for the Old Kent Road.

"In Churchill Walk for years the situation was this: my uncle George, that was my mother's step-brother, right? lived at 18 Churchill Walk. My auntie Rosie, that was my mother's step-sister, *one* of her step-sisters, right? lived upstairs in 11 Churchill Walk. My uncle Ken moved from 11 Churchill Walk to No. 4 Churchill Walk. When my father died, my *first* father that is, my mother moved to 4 Churchill Walk, upstairs on the top floor, right? My aunt Eileen came and lived in the middle floor of 4 Churchill Walk. My aunt Rosie and uncle Bill move from 11 Churchill Walk to No. 5 Churchill Walk. My cousin Helen, who was my grandmother's sister's daughter, my aunt Nell's daughter, moved to 11 Churchill Walk and lived upstairs where my aunt Rosie lived. My aunt Olive at one time lived in Churchill Walk—even me and Phyllis lived in Churchill Walk when we first got married."

Just as in Naples, this close community developed a dialect of its own. A Northern Italian moving south may at first think he is hearing his native language, but he will soon be at sea. I have seen an Englishman, born and brought up in Sussex, stare uncomprehendingly at a little Cockney boy asking for a penny to celebrate Guy Fawkes day. I had to translate.

A word of warning. Do not think that because you have seen Shaw's "Pygmalion" or its musical avatar, "My Fair Lady", even in the English language, you know what cockney sounds like. Shaw was Irish. Meeting him, it was always a little disconcerting to find how broad was his brogue; in moments of excitement, it sounded almost like stage Irish. The Cockney he gave Eliza was certainly stage cockney. To Shaw's ear, attuned to the music of Irish, the Cockney wailed up and down the scale like a cat on the tiles. He instructs his actress accordingly. But the Cockney does not whine: he (or she) speaks much too quickly for that. His elisions are more violent than those of Dante in the Divine Comedy. It is not enough to

Children walking under a wooden arch perpetuate the charity that a kind East End headmistress started in 1907. Any child with a farthing (a bronze coin worth a quarter of an old penny) who was still short enough to go under the arch got a "farthing bundle" of toys, containing much more than a farthing would buy. For taller children there was a penny bundle.

rhyme "rain" with "Rhine" as Shaw did. The connections must be mastered, as in the most exquisite Parisian French. "The rain in Spain lies mainly in the plain" becomes "Therhi Nin Spy Ner Ly zminely"—but I can go no further without the phonetic alphabet, and even the compilers of that boggle at cockney. Only once have I heard an actress on the West End stage risk real cockney, and she always made a little curtain-speech at the end to show she could really speak English.

To make things even more difficult, the Cockney invented a rhyming slang where new words replaced and utterly obscured the original. Thus a Cockney would say that his "plates of meat" hurt him, meaning his feet. And if you did not immediately understand him he would ask you to use your loaf. A loaf is, of course, made of bread, and bread rhymes with head. Elementary, of course, but I think it would have defeated Sherlock Holmes, at least for a while. He might, too, have been nonplussed if some-one from the Old Kent Road had confessed to beating his trouble-and-strife. But Holmes was not married.

I must emphasize that this curious way of talking had nothing secret about it. Part of the fun was to initiate the gentry (or "swells") into it, and to hear the pupil use it. If the Englishman is known for his reserve, the Cockney is noted for his open good-humour, which he can carry to the point of brashness. He is everybody's pal or chum or mate. When the startled foreigner is addressed as "dearie" or "ducks" or "love" by a waitress or barmaid he has known for less than a minute, then he is hearing the true sound of cockneydom. But let him beware. The out-and-out foreigner has always been considered by the Cockney as fair game for a minor swindle. London was the first city in the world to use the police to protect tourists. They stopped Cockney cab-drivers cheating visitors.

To someone who has lived in Europe, the Cockney has a strangely Continental *brio* and dash about him. He is extremely fond of family gatherings and he has a great gift for making a party go with a swing. He is as ready to burst into a song as any Italian: some of his Cockney songs are among the most rollicking ever written. Since they are meant to be sung by all present, women and children included, they are not indecent, although they may be coarse. Some have passed into the repertory of all classes. I have heard "My Old Man's a Dustman" roared out in a Bombay club while Indians listened, astonished, in the doorways. I have also soothed an alarmed *concierge* near the Roman Forum, and assured her that the fact that her tenants were shaking the floor to the tune of "Knees Up Mother Brown" did not mean that they were not as respectable as she had thought them to be. That particular dance and song is almost the anthem of the Cockneys.

The Cockney can be bawdy if he wants to and he prefers it done in a manner that makes the sly jokes of a "blue" comedian sound like an effeminate giggle. The Cockney invented that famous British institution, the Music Hall. The first one was opened in 1852, in Lambeth, the place of residence of Cockneys of the first water (and, incidentally, the Archbishop of Canterbury). The humour of the Music Hall was extremely broad. To give the patrons' lungs a rest, dance numbers were inserted between the items, and it was as a boy clog-dancer in one of these that Charlie Chaplin first came before the public. The Cockney Music Hall took England by storm, and crossed the Atlantic in a less robust form known as "Variety". It is a commonplace with writers about England to say that the Music Hall is dead. It is not dead yet. A young South African whom I met in my university days, Leonard Sachs, surprised me by saying that his one ambition was to revive it. This he did, acting, for a while, as the brazen, gavel-pounding Chairman himself. After many vicissitudes, he established his music hall as a London institution. His Victorian Late Joys can be seen in a small theatre near Charing Cross station. It should not be missed, if you can get a ticket.

The Music Hall threw up some of England's greatest theatrical personalities—Marie Lloyd, Albert Chevalier, George Robey and others. Their humour was that of the Cockney in the streets, to say nothing of the gutter. A Cockney delights in mimicking the accents (as near as he can) of the higher classes, which he finds hilarious. George Robey polished this device with great art. His raised eyebrows, his prim little expostulations, his shocked gestures as the audience roared at his Rabelaisian jokes, were a joy. "Desist", George Robey would plead with us, but we could not.

The Cockney had a Mediterranean taste for fiestas—days on which there is an excuse for doing nothing. They were not religious: Cockneys were as much a despair of earnest Christians as they were of the police. As Latin countries have the King and Queen of the Carnival, so the Cockneys had their Pearly King and Pearly Queen, often one of each neighbourhood. These arose from the habit of sewing pearl buttons on dresses and suits, a revolt against the drabness of Victorian men's costume and, perhaps, a forerunner of the Carnaby Street revolution. Celebrations consisted of outings. A favourite place was Hampstead Heath, a hilly open space in north-west London. There was a funfair, and a famous inn. But above all there was the darkness and, in one part of the Heath, some woods. Here couples enjoyed sex in an uninhibited fashion, long before various learned writers told us all how to follow suit. The inn was called "The Bull and Bush", and the goings on will be enshrined for as long as Londoners still sing together, in a famous song:

"Come, come, come and make eyes at me,
Down at the Old Bull and Bush."

The charm of the yokel is largely founded on the charm of his world: the farm, the village and the market town. His speech is that of his forebears. He is historically fascinating, like the village whipping post. Until the 1940s, that was true of the Cockney. [His world was that Churchill Walk that

Families share living space with chickens in the slums of the 1880s. As industry drew people to London, many thousands found there were not enough homes.

Allin has described.] If he went for a holiday, it was to the point of the English coast nearest to London—Southend, a place on the broad estuary of London's river, where the true sea is over a mile away at low tide. Here he went with his family on a day excursion, ate shell-fish, sang his songs, got drunk and danced "Knees Up Mother Brown". They were glorious sprees, vivid as no other jaunts were in the staid British Isles. They even gave a phrase to the language. Commentators on British television can be heard describing any gathering where dancing is the order of the day as a "knees-up"—even, ironically, an embassy ball.

Television—and there we have it. The Cockney had little use for its predecessor, radio. He talked too much himself to have time for listening. Besides, his favourite comedians did not come over well on the eyeless microphone. The nods, winks and wreathed smiles were lost: the Cockney accent was tinny on the primitive loudspeakers. That is, when it was heard at all. For its first decades, broadcasting was under the iron control of a high-minded Scotsman, John Reith, who was convinced that Marconi had been an agent of Heaven sent to civilize the English. The educated accent of the British Broadcasting Corporation was as repulsive to the Cockney as cockney had been to Bernard Shaw.

Then came television. Most of the British techniques were copied from the Americans, and with them came a Whitmanesque democracy. The man in the street was interviewed, and flattered by the interviewer. The life of the middle classes was brought into the narrow rooms of Churchill Walk. Family serials had the same grip upon the Cockney that the Victorian three-decker novels had once had upon his social betters.

The box triumphed, and not entirely because of its merits. We have seen how the bombing destroyed the slums, and what rose in their place. With the slum went the social life of the street corner, the alleyway, and the backyard fence. The Cockney stayed at home, learning how the other nine-tenths of the people lived.

Their children went to school, or were hauled into them by the scruff of their necks. Truancy, which had shaped the characters of their parents, now becomes no fun at all. It involved the descent of an army of social workers, fired with that passion only a little less ardent than that of the Christian missionary, the certainty that they knew best. Class-conscious school-teachers, remembering their own struggles to speak nicely, attacked the Cockney speech hip and thigh, believing it to be the product of ignorance and carelessness, when it was in fact a dialect as rigid as that of the Venetians or the Provençals. English, whether cockney, university, or pulpit, was once spoken in an even-toned rumble, very much as modern Hebrew is spoken by those who know it in Israel. But school-teachers must raise their voices to reach the back of the class, and with some men and most women this results in a squeak. Squeaking spread and is now endemic. The change was gradual and took decades, but now it is here to

Cockney's Rhyming Slang

Here are some examples of Cockney rhyming slang that have passed into general London parlance. The first few examples are sometimes used (often in an abbreviated form: "Let's have a butchers", "Use your loaf!") by people who are not even aware that originally they were rhyming slang.

Loaf of bread	—head
Butcher's hook	—look
Whistle and flute	—suit
Pig's ear	—beer
Apples and pears	—stairs
Boat-race	—face
Mutt and Jeff	—deaf
Pen and ink	—stink
Half-inch	—pinch (steal)
Pride and joy	—boy
East and West	—breasts
Bolt the door	—whore
Ham shank	—Yank (an American)
Horse and carts	—darts (pub game)
Mickey Mouse	—house
Noah's Ark	—nark (informer)
Sweeny Todd	—Flying Squad
Rosy Lea	—tea
Barnet Fair	—hair
Bees and honey	—money
(also "beez'un")	

stay. My attention was first drawn to it in Italy, where actors and others working to give an impression of the contemporary English speaker ran their voices up and down the scale like *coloratura* sopranos. Go to any great London store, listen, and hear English as it is spoken today by all save a few remaining Cockneys and, of course, the harassed Establishment.

But the Cockney survives, in a way—a ghostly way. Just as the European ghettoes survive in a turn of speech that suddenly surfaces in the smoothed-out civilization of New York, so the Cockney will unexpectedly emerge in London. He is no longer to be found in his old haunts. If you find people dancing "Knees Up Mother Brown" in a pub, they will be typists and bank clerks getting tipsy.

English conversation, as every visitor has found out, is dominated by the Gulf Stream. This body of water causes the English climate to be very changeable. To comment on it is compulsory. Everyone living in London for more than a few weeks will have made acquaintances with whom he discusses the weather, even if nothing else is said—the vendor of the evening newspaper, a barrow-boy selling fruit, the owner of a tiny tobacco shop. There is a way of talking about the weather that might with luck, unlock the cockney in them.

If the rain is pouring down in sheets and the newsvendor draws your attention to it, you must reply with Cockney optimism. Say, "Fine weather for ducks." An east wind is biting into your stomach. It is not "cold"; it is not "arctic"; it is not "damnable". It is "a bit parky". There has been rain, sleet, hail and snow for ten days. Say, "Ah well. Mustn't grumble." But if it is a day of unexpected sunshine in the midst of winter, reply with the immemorial wisdom of the poor, "Yes, you'll see, we'll have to pay for it," meaning that winter, like the rent collector, will soon be at the door again.

Persist in this, and perhaps you will have made a Cockney friend. If he is middle-aged, invite him one day to take a drink with you in the local pub. All the younger people there will be behaving with the desperate jollity of the advertisements on television. Select a quiet corner; fetch two pints of beer. Raise your glass to him, but no fashionable salutation is called for. A smile and a nod will do. Drink deep, lower your glass and say, "The beer isn't what it used to be." Then, if you are accepted, he will say, "Nothing is." And he is right. Churchill Walk is fast following its namesake to the grave.

Where the Street is a Stage

PHOTOGRAPHS BY LAURIE LEWIS

"Jumping Jack", once part of a famous dance trio and an old-timer of the West End, holds out a hat while tap-dancing to gramophone tunes outside a cinema.

From the time in the Middle Ages when the first tumblers came shouting and cartwheeling into the little town on the Thames, street entertainers have provided one of London's oldest and liveliest traditions. They are known as buskers—a word coming from the obsolete French verb *busquer*, for "beating the wood", making a noise to scare up game for the hunters. The London buskers' quarry is the passer-by with a little loose change to spare. Each busker works his own pitch, or territory, which may have been his for decades, and more than a few proclaim themselves to be the one and only "king of the buskers". Although their ranks have been joined lately by long-haired youths with guitars, most are proud of pasts that reach far back to music-hall days, and several of them were once quite well-known figures on the London stage.

The "Budgie Man" lectures his "disobedient" birds on their perch.

With a Little Help from the Birds

Buskers use all sorts of props, some of them live. The "Budgie Man" (left) has taught his budgerigars a comic act: they ignore their master's commands for tricks until the audience answers his plea to shout. Then he sounds a police siren and they rush for their cage. The street musician above cranks his machine and attracts extra attention with his parrot.

With parrot and polyphone—an old music-box playing perforated discs—this Portobello Road regular attracts the tourists at the outdoor antique market.

A shirtless busker cuffs and insults his defenceless partner, calling him "you horrible, miserable worm", to stimulate the audience before the act commences.

Tied up in a sack and loaded with chains, the escape artist writhes around, finds an opening and slithers free.

A Gruesome Display

Near the Tower of London an act reminiscent of medieval torture combined with black humour is played a dozen times a day. An escapologist wriggles from a chain-wrapped canvas bag, but the real star is the man who adds gruesome drama by taunting and slapping him. The make-believe bully also threatens spectators with curses if they do not pay up when the act is over. He may even pierce his own cheeks with a pin to keep the crowd's attention.

In Petticoat Lane's crowded Sunday market, browsers and shoppers are serenaded by a blind singer and his companion playing determinedly on the accordion.

Pedlars of Music

Some of the oldest and best-loved of London's street musicians
are found in the East End. They depend for their pennies not on
affluent tourists so much as on people often little better off
than themselves. Londoners of all classes make a point of paying
the busker—at times for a favourite tune, but also to ensure
that his music will continue to be heard in the streets.

In Club Row market a former music-hall star, known as "The Caruso Clown and his one-stringed fiddle", supports himself against a wall as he bows to a donor.

With a deep concentration the crouching artist works on a new picture.

Pavement Rembrandt

Working appropriately near the National Gallery, an artist applies years of experience and dozens of deft strokes and smudges of chalk to paving stones, producing idyllic scenes that bring the coins clinking down. Pavement artists are not, strictly speaking, buskers, but their work has basically the same purpose—to sell ephemeral pleasure to anybody who wants it.

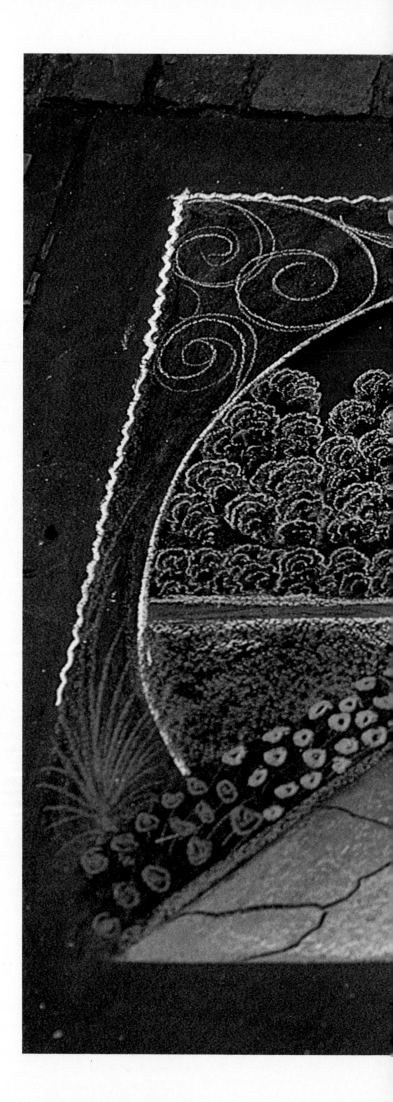

This landscape cannot be hung, taken home or sold. At the end of the day it will be rubbed out by the artist, who will create another the following day.

8

The Capital City

I have said that the Londoner dislikes labels for his city. But there is one he might have used, if luck had not gone against him. Less than a century ago, those who knew Latin did use it, at least in the sanctuary of the libraries. *Caput mundi*: the head of the world. There have been only two cities in the whole of history that could claim that title: Rome, which once ruled all the Western world, and London, which once was the capital city of three-quarters of the terrestrial globe.

Rome has its ruins, and since the Middle Ages thoughtful people from Petrarch to Henry James have mused over them. The usual thoughts were to contrast Rome's past glory with its present. Nobody, except the transient Mussolini, has ever thought that Rome would once more be the *caput mundi*. With London it is different. The days of its empire are so recent, the loss of it so sudden, that a feeling of *caput mundi* remains in many of its citizens. *London Pride* is the name of a modest little plant that grows in rockeries. The pride of a Londoner is equally unobtrusive, but it is there. We shall now seek its monuments.

We begin at Charing Cross. It was here that Dr. Johnson said he felt the full tide of life. He was lucky; today we can only feel the full tide of the traffic, and if the Doctor had walked with his uncertain gait in its streets today, his life would have come to a very rapid ebb. We must bolt underground, nose our way through a warren of tunnels, and come out through that rabbit hole marked "To Whitehall". Taking our lives in our hands, we cross the road to an island on which stands the statue of a man who lost his life not far away: Charles I. It is the most beautiful statue in London's open-air, and it is by a Frenchman, Hubert Le Sueur. Charles sits astride a magnificent horse, and on the pavement behind the horse's ample rump is a plaque. This plaque marks the official centre of London. All distances are measured from here. Rome, too, had its marker from which the miles to its distant frontiers were measured. Rome's marker is a grandiose affair of marble and bronze. This one is as much more modest as London's empire was much more vast.

From Whitehall we can look down a great perspective of buildings as big as palaces, ending in a great array of Gothic spires. Turning, we find another noble panorama: a square with statues and fountains, and a huge column with Nelson on the top. This is Trafalgar Square. If we muse at all amid the traffic, it must be to think that, had all London been as magnificent as this, Rome would have been outdone. It was once London's intention that it should be so.

Beneath the bulk of an imperial crown adorning a gate to St. James's Park, resourceful sparrows make themselves at home in the formal leaves of Edwardian stonework. In the park's green interior nest 17 species of birds.

There is another modest monument across Trafalgar Square. In the pavement on the north side are set rods of bronze. They are the Imperial Standards of Length: an inch, a foot, a yard, and a chain. They are the most awkward standards that can be imagined. The yard, for instance, is said to be the distance between the tip of the nose of some forgotten king and the ends of his fingers with his arm outstretched. They have been the cause of tears among schoolchildren plentiful enough to fill the ornamental basins on either side of these rods. Still, awkward or not, they were Imperial standards, and men of all hues and a hundred faiths had to use them. Those Colonials, the Americans, still do.

Rome's empire slowly declined over the centuries: London's keeled over in a matter of years. The foot, the yard, the inch were seen for what they were: an exasperation to foreigners. They were dropped—just as the sixpence, the shilling and the half-crown were. The change was so swift that many a man who sweated at school over the Imperial measures, lived to see his first child skip happily through the metric system.

I played my small part in the fall of the British Empire, a feeble tug on one of the ropes that pulled down the colossus; and I played that part here in the square. The base of Nelson's column is an ample plinth guarded by four bronze lions. Between these animals there is a sort of sanctuary of liberty. It is the site of demonstrations that have altered history. It is the place where you can say, at the top of your voice, what you please, provided you are serious in your intent and have an organization behind you that the police can name in their blotters. (If you are on your own, you go to Speaker's Corner in Hyde Park; but that spot, so beloved of foreign reporters, is merely a joke for cranks. In recent years no serious politician has ever spoken there.)

In the company of Members of Parliament and men who would one day be rulers of their distant lands, I took my turn, in my younger years, in denouncing the Empire to large crowds bearing banners. It was a thrilling experience, unless, as often happened, you saw people on the edge strolling off to feed the pigeons. Having said my say, I would repose against one of the lions. On reflection, while I am convinced that our demonstrations had some effect on Parliament's gradual dissolution of the Empire, I do not know that I learned as much about politics in Trafalgar Square as I did about art: I recall being continuously lost in wonder at how Sir Edwin Landseer, the sculptor of the figures in the Square, could be so incompetent.

Years later, after the Second World War, I passed by Trafalgar Square again. Landseer's lions were unscathed. But at the base of the column were gigantic placards which read EXPORT OR DIE. They were reminders that the Empire was rapidly vanishing. England now stood alone. She would have to earn her living by the sweat of her own brow. It was a lesson that, even 30 years after the end of the war, had still not been fully learned.

The 100,000 people who flocked to Trafalgar Square (above) in 1843, when Nelson's memorial was erected, were the last to have a close look at the statue. Since then, high up on top of its 170-foot column, it has been inspected only by the square's famous pigeons and a few stonework cleaners. In the picture (right) a telescopic lens gives a rare view of London's least seen cliché.

I have said that many Londoners still feel some sense of the days of Empire. But, of course, no true Londoner would let himself get carried away by it. In my boyhood there were White Russians, gentle and tearful people who, in return for a meal, would mourn the fall of the Czars most picturesquely. There are no White Englishmen; or if there are any, they will soon be dead and gone.

Instead, the Londoner has written his own version of history. As you would expect from the city of Shakespeare and talented actors, it is most dramatic—much more so, perhaps, than the real thing.

The Londoner has fixed—and it is part of the folklore of the city—on a month and a date: August, 1914. It was, according to the records, rather a hot summer, but that sun has gilded a whole period. It was the Golden Age, from which by the sword of war the English were driven from Paradise, never to return. "Golden Ages" are, of course, nonsense. But it happened that the beginning of the 20th Century produced a master of nonsense. England's Golden Age is perfectly reflected in the novels of P. G. Wodehouse. He set his stories in various decades, no doubt obedient to the demands of publishers, but all his characters live and move in that mythical Eden "before nineteen fourteen". I have seen Londoners grow moist-eyed while listening to songs they could not have heard even in the womb. British television, while flailing the present English world with bitter sarcasm, scored its greatest success of the Seventies with a series portraying the world before 1914 as seen both by servants and master, and it was all what the Americans call "gracious", as much in the downstairs kitchen as the upstairs drawing-room.

There is a monument that is a sort of boundary stone between this Golden Age and what was to come: a marker of the beginning of bleaker times. To find it we must turn our backs on the Imperial Standard Measure, pass the plinth where the agitators gathered, regain the horse that presents its rump to London's centre, and go down the street at which it points its head. On either side the palaces of Whitehall rear their domes and turrets into the sky. Halfway down there is a white construction, diminutive against the great façades, and made of marble. Some wreaths and flowers lie against its base. In shape it is one oblong box placed upon a bigger one. In design it is said to be Greek, although it derives from nowhere but its architect's limited imagination. At least it has a Greek name. It is the Cenotaph, or an empty tomb. On its sides flags droop above the traffic. The figures "1914-1918" were carved upon it when it was first put up, and then, later, "1939-1945". It was intended as a reminder of the dead in what was called the Great War, and at first Londoners took off their hats when they passed it, even if they were on the top deck of a bus. Nowadays, except on one day of the year, nobody gives it a second glance. The passer-by needs no monument to remind him that his country lost two wars while heroically winning them.

In florid Victorian Gothic style, the fretted canopy of the Albert Memorial rises from behind a cluster of the blandly sculptured figures that are liberally distributed throughout the monument's design. The elaborate structure, built mainly of white marble and pink granite and adorned with bright mosaics, houses a 14-foot bronze statue of the Prince Consort.

Let us emulate our contemporaries, pass on, and look about us. From Nelson on his pillar to the far end of the street, where the huge, hunched figure of Winston Churchill makes a gloomy silhouette of bronze against the palaces, all around us lies the evidence, of power and glory. It is the evidence of that past pride the Londoner once put in his Dominion "over palm and pine", as the song goes, a pride many foreigners found as exasperating as the yard and inch. Let us see how these buildings arose.

When, in the middle of the 19th Century, money began to pour into London from all over the world, Londoners began to realize that they had not much to show that their city was *caput mundi*. Rome had its Colosseum, its Forum of Trajan, and the forest of marble pillars on the Palatine, the hill that gave the world the word for "palace". London had no real palace. There had been one in Whitehall, but it had been burned down and not rebuilt. The residence of the monarch was only a nobleman's town residence, which the knowledgeable around the Court called, correctly, "Buck House". There was Westminster Abbey, and a long way away, St. Paul's, but nothing particularly striking in between. Something had to be done about it. Buildings must be built. But what *sort* of buildings? Over this question there arose a quarrel, to which London owes a great deal of its variety. From the Great Fire until just before the age of Victoria, there was only one way to put up a building, and that, as we have seen, was to copy the Italians. This had given London St. Paul's. Yet there was Westminster Abbey, on the other side of the city, all spikes and pointed arches. St. Paul's was impressive, but the Abbey was romantic. St. Paul's spoke of the Latins, but the Abbey was redolent of the novels of Sir Walter Scott. The Victorians grew rich in the most prosaic way imaginable—through trade and machinery. Just as the 20th Century took refuge from its dullness in the dream-world of Hollywood, so the Victorians found solace in a dream-world of the Middle Ages.

As I have suggested, architects are creatures of their times. Since the Middle Ages were fashionable among the rich (and they were very rich) of industrial Britain, some architects turned their attention to the building tastes of those admired times. They studied the Gothic style. Originally the word was a rude one: the Gothic style—all gloom and stained glass— was considered in the 18th Century as barbarian, something only suitable for the Goths. But now it seemed to have new merits. It was morally elevating: nowhere could one feel so much above the sordid cares of the market-place as when one was craning one's neck to look up at a shadowy vault. Moreover, in a way, it was the only truly English style. The French had invented it, but England had adopted it, and the country was dotted with Gothic cathedrals, some of them equal to, if not better than, anything the French could do. Besides, the English had invented a version of Gothic all their own: English Perpendicular, so called for its tall and narrow windows and its severe restraint, was a very British style.

Photographed from an unfamiliar angle between groups of statuary, the Royal Albert Hall's giant rotunda, 700 feet in circumference, looms over a modern pair of admiring lovers. While notable for poor acoustics, the hall's glass-domed interior space—it can hold 8,000 people—and its years of tradition have made it one of London's most popular concert halls.

At the same time, other architects stuck firmly to the Latin fashion, and thus a great fight arose. Fortunately, it was not merely between professors of art, but between architects of considerable gifts. In one corner was Augustus Pugin, defender of the Gothic style and very capable of striking a shrewd blow. St. Peter's, Rome, was the apex of the Latin style. Pugin detested it. One day he was found on his knees in the basilica. Rising, he told his companion that he was thanking the Almighty because he had detected a crack in the dome. In the other corner was Sir Charles Barry, classical to his finger-tips. Not only did he design the finer buildings of Pall Mall, he also laid out Trafalgar Square.

The Victorians never made up their minds about the quarrel. They leaned first one way, and then the other. For instance, Queen Victoria wanted to build a monument to her husband, Prince Albert. The result was the Albert Memorial. In my youth this was derided as an example of Victoria's appallingly bad taste. Later in life, I was curious enough to go into the original documents about its building. It turned out that she had very good taste indeed. What she wanted was an enormous monolithic obelisk, made of granite; it would have looked something like the Washington Monument. The whole affair was to be paid for by public subscription. There is in existence a large bound volume presented to Her Majesty by the Committee, in which they tell her unequivocally that the public had not come forth with enough money to pay for the cost of hewing and transporting such a monster. She had to settle for the less ambitious but more fashionable—and far fussier—Gothic. Thus to this day, Prince Albert of Saxe-Coburg sits under an ornate canopy, as Gothic as it could be made, clutching a book I was always told was the Bible, but which is in fact the catalogue of the Great Exhibition held in the Crystal Palace.

But the classicists also had their day. The canopy is surrounded by a bas-relief containing no fewer than 178 figures, all done in the *classical* style. Furthermore, at the angles of the plinth are groups of free-standing figures that would have passed muster, so far as style was concerned, with the Emperor Constantine. He might, however, have been disconcerted by their subjects: Manufacture, Engineering, Commerce and Agriculture.

In 1834 the quarrel came to a head, to London's great benefit. At first the blessing was well disguised. The Houses of Parliament had burned down. There was money galore to put them up again, but in which style should the thing be done? Gothic would be fashionable and English; it would also be extremely uncomfortable for the Commons and the Lords, and especially for the Speaker, who lives there. The spacious Latin style, favoured by the monarchs for their palaces, would seem to be necessary for all the comings and goings that governing a country required. The result was a typically English compromise—and a masterpiece. Barry was asked to plan the building; Pugin was commissioned to make it look Gothic. The result is the Palace of Westminster, at the end of Parliament

In the refreshment room of the Victoria and Albert Museum a ceramic frieze in decorated capitals runs all the way round the four walls. The word BETTER is from the motto: "There is nothing better for a man than that he should eat and drink and that he should make his soul enjoy good in his labour." The frieze was done in 1871 by students of the Royal College of Art, next door to the museum.

Street, with its Victoria Tower, its central pinnacle, and the fantasy of the clock-tower with Big Ben, the name not of the clock but of the bell that strikes the hours. Barry designed a plan that still serves, it was so convenient. Pugin designed every little detail, down to the inkstands. He was thorough. He lamented that the furniture had not the patina that real Gothic furniture had acquired, but with magnificent Victorian confidence he was sure that it would acquire it with the passage of the centuries. Alas for Pugin! It has been busily scraped and re-varnished in our own hygienic times, no doubt with some new plastic.

The odd combination of these two men produced a triumph. The Houses of Parliament is the biggest Gothic palace in the world, and by far the most impressive. The palace of the Popes at Avignon looks skimpy beside it. Barry's plan gives it a dozen surprising perspectives, something that Gothic cathedrals sometimes lack. Inside it is as functional as anything in steel and concrete. Lords, Commons, Kings and Queens move about it with ease and dignity. Perhaps the greatest tribute to Barry was paid after the Second World War. A bomb had destroyed the House of Commons—the principal chamber in the whole complex. The House had not quite enough seats for all the representatives of contemporary Britain. But is was so perfect as a debating chamber that it was decided to rebuild it exactly the same size. The new chamber is also, in a left-handed way, a tribute to Pugin. An attempt was made to copy his decoration. It was quite a worthy effort, but anybody who knew the old chamber can feel his absence like a chill breeze. In his own time Pugin himself had dismissed the whole vast enterprise as a muddle. "All Grecian, Sir", he once said. "Tudor details on a classic body."

The new *caput mundi* could very well have been built wholly in the Gothic taste. In that case, Whitehall would have looked like two rows of cathedrals. It is a beguiling thought: on a misty October morning, London would have had the most beautiful prospect of any great city in the world. It was not to be. The Latinists had their way. The architecture of Rome was, after all, the most satisfactory expression of pomp and power. So, instead of cathedrals, Whitehall is today lined with Italianate palaces. The believers in Gothic continued to put up a grand fight. Pugin's successor was George Gilbert Scott. He was asked to build a new Foreign Office, worthy of the city that headed the most powerful nation on earth. He drew up a Gothic design, but it was not accepted. He was not to be defeated. With some changes, he used the design to build, of all things, a new railway station. St. Pancras terminus is still there, with a three-hundred-foot tower that splendidly and arrogantly serves no purpose at all, except to look beautiful. The lovers of Gothic had a final triumph, before 1914 and the war put an end to the Golden Days. The Royal Courts of Justice in the Strand contains a Gothic hall fit for a medieval Pope. The rest of the building, say the lawyers who have to use it, is not at all fit for them.

The soldiers came back from the Great War—that is, the First World War as we now call it. They had left singing, "Keep the Home Fires Burning"; they came back singing an ironical little ditty that went, "It wasn't the Yanks who won the war, it was my son Billy." And it wasn't the British Prime Minister who dominated the Peace Conference, but an American called Wilson. London still claimed to be the world's greatest city, but it looked uneasily across the Atlantic at a rival, New York, where towers were rising quicker than trees in a forest, and a good deal taller than three hundred feet. Soon businessmen were jumping off those towers, but that brought little solace to London. The Slump, as Londoners called the great Depression, spread to their own city.

London's days as *caput mundi* were at an end. But the way in which London fell from her post as the world's first city also gave her some of her most splendid days. The Second World War broke out, and London was relentlessly bombed, first by aeroplanes, then by flying bombs and rockets. Thirty thousand people died; 50,000 were injured; acres of the town were devastated; the Guildhall itself, which had burned in the Great Fire, burned again. Night after night, Londoners slept in air raid shelters or the Underground. When the bombing began, no one knew what the outcome would be. Amid the stomach-churning roar of the bombs, the immense flames that sucked the very air from the streets, the crash of buildings and the shrieks of the injured, it seemed each night that London must die.

Yet each morning came the miracle. Londoners emerged from their shelters, picked their way over the debris, and quietly went about their business. Commuters in the suburbs, who could see the sky red with destruction over the City, got up as usual, kissed their wives and caught the usual train. Often, when they arrived at their shops and offices, they found nothing but a hole in the ground. They waited patiently until some-one told them where to go. Churchill, with all his gift of phrase, never found one to describe this astonishing calm, although it was happening all around him. The citizens found their own: "London can take it."

It is hard to believe, but true, that Londoners grew almost *bored* with the bombing. Not, of course, with the actual raids. There was, as they said, plenty of variety, from bombs that whistled, landmines that destroyed whole blocks, incendiary-bomb raids that set ten thousand conflagrations in ten minutes—and the flying bombs, a true test of nerves, because you were safe while you could hear them, but when the noise stopped as the engine cut out, the silence meant that in the next second you could well be dead. No: the boredom came from everybody having his or her "bomb story". This the Londoner found a sore trial. In the end the listener would groan when confronted with another bomb story, as when confronted with a bad pun.

The war ended. The new dates were carved on the Cenotaph, new buildings arose over the holes in the ground. London had held its head high, but it was no longer *caput mundi*. Then there arose a feeling that must forever remain a mystery to the foreigner, a mystery indeed even to me, who had not been there during the bombing: Londoners began to treasure the memory of it. Peace came, and lasted. It brought its blessings, but it also brought a world in which each man was for himself. Men and women went daily to work as they had done when they picked their way over shattered glass and over the blood-stains. But now rat eyed rat as each endeavoured to keep ahead in the race. Londoners forgot the smoke and the horror; instead, they recalled the days when each man helped his neighbour, when Londoners could not only take, but give. Something of the comradeship of the slums that I have described had spread over the entire city during those hours of trial. Londoners are sorry it has gone.

Gone for ever, because London itself has changed. The Empire dissolved, but for the first time Londoners saw and rubbed shoulders with the people they had governed. Immigrants from India, Pakistan, the West Indies and other places in that imperium on which the sun never set, poured into a London on which, it seemed to them, the sun rarely rose. They took possession of whole areas. Londoner meeting Londoner in suburban streets that might have been Harlem would wryly raise his hat and say, "Dr. Livingstone, I presume." But they soon grew tired of patronizing jokes. Now they have accepted the fact that the new London is a "multi-racial" city, a term coined by the sociologists which has no real meaning for the true Londoner. He waits for the children of the immigrants to grow up, and he waits to see what sort of people they will be. He has no great faith in the melting pot. Does it mean he will have to melt too?

In the archives of the Victoria and Albert Museum is a series of drawings. They were made by architects when London led the world, and they were made in the faith that her supremacy, like that of Rome, would last for centuries. They are of great buildings, some fantastically Gothic, some majestic in the Italian style. They show a bubbling creative spirit, a leaping ambition to build a city all of which would be as impressive as the Palace of Westminster, with perspectives as noble as that of Whitehall. They have one thing in common. None of the designs was ever built. And now they never will be.

Still, when the Londoner walks across Trafalgar Square, down Whitehall, and past the sculptured flanks of the Palace of Westminster, he is proud of what once was, and muses upon what might have been.

Landmarks Aglow with Tradition

PHOTOGRAPHS BY PATRICK THURSTON

While it shares an aura of medievalism with the almost 900-year-old Tower of London (left), Tower Bridge (above) is in fact a feat of Victorian engineering.

London's architectural images are so deeply imprinted on the world's mind that people who have never been within thousands of miles of the Thames instantly recognize this scene of the medieval Tower and adjacent Tower Bridge. (Indeed, so familiar is the bridge that some mistakenly think of it as London Bridge, which is further upriver.) Many of London's landmarks have been surrounded by glass and steel monoliths. But the city fathers have compensated by floodlighting the monuments, with the result that the best time to appreciate London now is at night. When darkness cloaks the new high-rise buildings, the city's historic edifices and memorials quietly reassume their rightful prominence, and their floodlit magnificence is assurance that even in an era of rapid architectural change, London's proudest structures remain inviolate.

From 170 feet up Nelson scans Trafalgar Square, named for the naval victory in which he died.

Reminders of a Triumphant Past

The empire that made London capital of the world was won in many a battle, and a grateful nation honoured her heroes with adulation. None received more glory than Nelson and Wellington, who at the beginning of the 19th Century defeated France at sea and on land, assuring Britain's mastery of the globe for the next hundred years. Their victories are still recorded in bronze and stone.

At Hyde Park Corner an arch celebrates Wellington's Waterloo triumph; in the foreground a memorial honours First World War artillerymen.

Spires of the Houses of Parliament are seen from across the river.

Houses of Power

London has not one but two grand seats of government. The Palace of Westminster that houses Parliament is known to every tourist. Just across the river is County Hall, less well known but in many ways equally important to the capital's citizens. From there the Greater London Council governs the city, operating on a budget larger than those of some nations.

Sprawling like the vast metropolis it runs, County Hall covers about six and a half acres on the south bank of the river. Part of it dates from 1912.

Wren's masterpiece, St. Paul's Cathedral, no longer London's tallest building, still dominates the skyline.

Soaring Shrines of Britain's Faith

Only one of the capital's two great churches, St. Paul's, belongs to the city. The other, Westminster Abbey, is a Royal Peculiar, which means—theoretically at least—that it is the special preserve of the monarch, who appoints its officials. For 900 years most British rulers have been crowned in the Abbey, and until 1760 most were interred there. More than five million visitors a year view the memorials to the famous that crowd the aisles.

Although begun by Edward the Confessor in 1050, most of the Abbey's structure dates from the 13th Century. The twin towers were added in the 18th Century.

9

The Pride of the Londoner

We are near the end of our journey. We have tramped the streets of the City (the secret of enjoying London is to walk), the East and West Ends and the quiet squares; we have gone North and South and, at last, find ourselves outside the Houses of Parliament. We must go inside. Only by doing that can we understand why the Londoner, his city twice burned down, his dominion gone with the snows of yesterday, is still quietly proud.

He is proud because here, or within a few hundred yards of this building, from the days of Simon de Montfort, a system of democratic government was slowly hammered out. Here a way was discovered, after countless trials and errors, by which people could govern themselves. If Athens and Rome gave us our civilization, London gave us that thing without which civilization has no meaning—namely, freedom.

As we approach we see that the House of Commons is sitting. We know that because, if it is day, a Union Jack flies above the clock-tower; if it is night, a bright light burns at the top. We ask a policeman if we can see what is going on, and we are politely waved inside. We are directed to a place called St. Stephen's chapel, which is not a chapel at all, but a waiting room. We gaze forlornly at some frescoes that are even worse than Landseer's lions. We wait until we are beckoned by an attendant. We follow him meekly. It is all rather like a Pall Mall Club, and so it should be, because the House of Commons has been called the best club in the world.

We have waited because we are strangers. If we are that key figure in this club, the common voter, we can send a summons to our own Member. If we have addressed meetings to get him elected, or even envelopes, he will soon come down to greet us. After all, a Prime Minister, Ramsay Macdonald, began his political life by addressing envelopes. In that case we shall be shown into a lofty, Gothic place called the Central Lobby. Here we will meet our own Member or, with luck, the Prime Minister himself.

Perhaps, if we are early, and the House is preparing to get down to business, we shall hear a rather alarming cry echoing round the vault. "Mr. Speaker! Hats—off—strangers!" We take off our hats, if we have any, or just stand and gape respectfully. A little procession sweeps rapidly through the Central Lobby. There is a man in knee-breeches carrying a great golden mace on his shoulder. He is the Sergeant-at-Arms. Beware: if we shout a rude slogan, he can lock us up in a special cell in the Victoria Tower. Behind him comes a man wearing a black robe laced with gold and a prickly-looking greyish wig down to his shoulders. He is the Speaker. He is called that because centuries ago he was appointed to speak to the sovereign when that august person asked for money from the taxes. His duty was to convey the comments of the Commons, most of whom would have had their hearts in their mouths when faced with their liege lord, to say nothing of his headsman. It was a dangerous job. When the Speaker was elected to office, he was led to his chair. On the way he made little struggles with his sponsors to show it was a job he did not want. It is still a job that not everyone would take. There is no danger to his neck these days, but it is hard on his bottom. He has to sit for hours on a straight-backed chair and listen to interminable speeches and pretend to have no opinion about them. He is one of the most important persons in the Realm, but any quizmaster who asked contestants to name him would be ruled unfair. The Speaker has apartments in the Palace of Westminster, and his life is lived entirely among politicians. In compensation for this fate, he can drive to a coronation in a coach bigger than that of the monarch.

He is followed by a train-bearer, a chaplain and a secretary. He disappears into the House. By devious routes, we follow him. But we must wait a little. The chaplain is leading the House of Commons in prayers to Almighty God to give them wisdom. We are not allowed in. A cynical journalist who had spent 12 years reporting the proceedings has given his opinion that this is precisely the moment when every voter should join in on bended knees; but it is not permitted.

At last we are shown into a high gallery, by a man in evening dress with a great gold badge dangling over his stomach. In spite of his resemblance to a sommelier, he does not offer us the wine menu; instead he gives us, free, the programme of the day. We note that somebody is going to ask the Prime Minister a question. Eagerly we look below us to spot the Prime Minister.

I have seen the President of the United States address a joint session of Congress, and what struck me most was the profound respect with which he was greeted on his entrance. A flunkey bawled his title; all rose, some

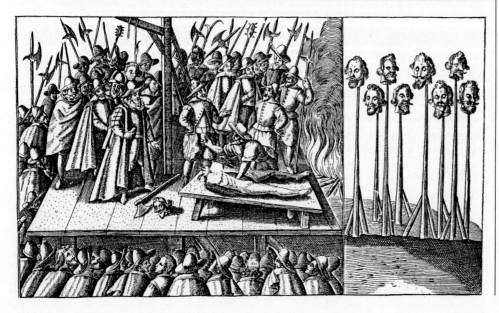

Guy Fawkes's attempt to blow up King James I in Parliament in November 1605 ended with punishment by beheading for the conspirators. This engraving of 1606 shows five of the eight victims being dragged to the scaffold (left), the execution of one (centre) and the eight skewered heads displayed on stakes (right).

Ranks of coathangers in the cloakroom of the House of Commons still have dangling red tapes that were once used by Members of Parliament to hang up their swords before they entered the Chamber of the House for debates.

applauded while the President, bestowing smiles upon the favoured, made a regal progress down the aisle. In the House, the Prime Minister slips in from behind the Speaker's chair as unobtrusively as a boy late for school. He takes his seat on a bench, as others shift to make room for him.

The House is divided into two sets of parallel benches, with a table in between on which has been put the mace. On the carpet are two red lines, one for each side. Tradition has it that Members may not cross these lines, lest they should come to fisticuffs. Nowadays they occasionally do cross it. Once a Member even ran away with the mace because he disagreed with one of the Speaker's rulings. But generally they do not cross. Instead, Members on the Front Benches—that is, those who lead the Government and Opposition—throw little notes across to their opponents, again very like school, except that the Speaker does not keep them in after lessons.

We have been told to take off our hats. We now observe a Member hastily clapping one on his head. He rises and says, "Mr. Speaker, on a point of order," and everything stops. The hat is obligatory. Members have been known to borrow one, or even make one out of the programme of the day. Keir Hardie, the first working man to get elected, in 1892, caused a sensation by wearing a cloth cap. He was well-liked for it, as well he might have been, for he founded the Independent Labour Party which, as the Labour Party pure and simple, was later to govern the country.

The debate of the day begins. It may be something that will affect the destiny of the nation for centuries to come; but if we expect to hear the thunders of Gladstone or Disraeli, we shall be disappointed. In truth, we do not really know what those two sounded like in the Commons. Edmund Burke, who reads tremendously in print, is said to have had a very poor delivery. I myself as a schoolboy heard Churchill defend his Budget from

In order to relieve the repetitive regularity of black-painted iron railings at each front door in Trevor Place, off Knightsbridge, one of the householders has set out a bright window-box full of frilly pink petunias.

the Front Bench and, as a young man, sat three weeks in the Strangers' Gallery hearing him fight the India Bill clause by clause. On no occasion did he stir me, or anybody else. The House prefers a pedestrian way of talking. It dislikes being exhorted; it refuses to be browbeaten. It permits a very few favourites to have a silver tongue. Lloyd George was one of them, but he spent most of his life out of office.

We must not, then, expect to hear a Demosthenes or a Cicero. We shall not hear a Danton either. There is no drama. There is a debate, and sometimes it would seem that a Member opposing a measure has irrefutable arguments. It does not matter. The result of the debate has been fixed in advance. If foreigners find this peculiar, a new Member often finds it violently frustrating. He has promised his electors a hundred things, from Utopia to a new housing estate. He glows with the feeling that he is one of the six hundred or so men who govern the Realm. He makes his first speech. It is called his "maiden" speech, and in it he can say pretty well what he likes. After that, the maiden is introduced in no uncertain manner to the facts of life.

He belongs to one of the political parties in the House, since independents are nowadays very rare birds; and he is expected to vote with the other members of his party. Each party has gentlemen known expressively as Whips. The name comes from the hunting-field. The Whips are employed to whip back into the pack any hound that tries to stray. The new Member soon learns to come to heel. On any important matter, the Chief Whip issues a notice that is an order to vote exactly as the party wishes. If the order has three lines under it, the new Member will disobey it at his peril. He will at such a time be called up in front of the Whips and he will be given a stern dressing-down. He cannot salve his conscience by playing truant. If he has urgent business elsewhere and the Government majority in the House is slim, he will be forced to "pair"—that is, to find someone in the opposing party who also does not want to vote because he has urgent business elsewhere. Pairs are not always easy to find. Unpaired Members who were sick have been carried in on stretchers to record their "Aye" or "Nay".

New Members, their dream of governing Great Britain fading, have been known to subside into long sulks during which they do not say a word. Others set about learning the game, a process which may take months. Debates, the new Member finds, are fixed beforehand by the big Parliamentary guns, in little chats behind the Speaker's Chair. He eagerly seizes upon Question Time, which takes place every day. Here anybody, new boy or not, can ask a Minister almost any question he chooses. But even in this case there are rules, some of them maddeningly intricate. Suppose, for instance, the Member is boiling to ask the Chancellor of the Exchequer a question about the Member's own constituency, Muddleton-on-Sea. If the question does not precisely concern that Minister, the Minister will promptly pass the buck to someone else. The frustrated Member will resume his seat. Perhaps then some older hand will helpfully nudge him and whisper, "Visit, visit." So he rises again. He reframes his question. "Does the Right Honourable Member", he asks the Chancellor, "intend to visit Muddleton-on-Sea, and if he does, will he take notice of the scandalous action . . . " and so forth. At least, the problem has been aired and the question will go down in the daily record for him to show his constituents.

There are a hundred other things he has to learn, and one of them is modesty. If, when he catches the Speaker's eye, he rises to make that speech that brought the audience cheering to its feet back in Muddleton, and he finds he is addressing only 14 Members, two of whom are asleep, he must grin and bear it. He slowly realizes that *he* is certainly not governing the country, but the House of Commons *is*.

It may take months; but gradually the new Member learns how things get done. He may not be listened to with any great attention when he gets on his feet to address the House. But upstairs, in the Committee Rooms where new laws are examined clause by clause by small groups of Members, he will one day find, to his pleasure, that some commonsense amendment of his is willingly adopted by the Government. As his reputation grows as a "good Commons man", his opinion will be sought over drinks at the bar, in the lounge and in the corridors. He will learn to use in conversation the magic phrase: "When I was last in my constituency, they were telling me that . . . .". And Ministers will lend him an ear. That is because every Member of the House, however great and powerful, must listen to what the country is saying. If they do not, at the next election they may no longer be Members of the best club in the world.

And here is the heart of the matter. Here is why London is a proud city, even in its decline from glory. In modern times, when men sought to rid themselves of the tyranny of kings or dictators, their thoughts often turned to London, the place where representative government, by and for the people, was shown to be possible. London was the place where it *worked*. It was an example that spread across the world. It was copied, sometimes with success, sometimes not. But wherever true democracy took root and flourished, that country owes a debt to London.

But let me temper that statement with true London reserve. I do not mean that the parliamentary system owes its origin only to the London citizen. To the contrary. The constitution of Great Britain was built up piece by piece by country gentlemen who, like the rest of us even today, disliked paying their taxes and had a shrewd suspicion that, when they did, a great deal of their money was squandered. But to keep a check on this they came to London, to Westminster, to deliberate in peace.

The London citizenry was, and is, a peaceable lot. Surveying its history, one is struck by the fact that there have been so few riots, and not one wholesale insurrection. There have been invasions, always brief, by malcontents from the countryside; but there has been only one local trouble of

Only yards from London's traffic, children play in a secluded bosky garden in the middle of Bryanston Square, in the heart of the city. Although several of the larger garden squares are public, many others—like this one—remain the cherished privilege of the occupants of the surrounding houses.

any consequence: the Gordon riots of the 18th Century, an affair of religious prejudice, and soon over. Indeed, the riots would have been forgotten had they not taken place when London was blessed with pamphleteers of considerable literary skill. Otherwise, while Parliament quarrelled with the King and both sides went to war, London went about its business, which was, as Dr. Johnson described it, that most innocent of human occupations, making money.

Londoners never stormed the Bastille, as the Parisians did, nor took the roof off a conclave of cardinals to force them to elect a Pope, as once happened in Rome. True, they approved of the beheading of Charles I, and packed Whitehall to see the show. Equally, when they had got tired of the Cromwellians, they came out into the streets to welcome another Charles back to the throne. But there has never been an anti-government demonstration in London equal to those of the late 1960s in Washington over the Vietnam war. The small boy who asked my friend for a penny for the "Guy" recalls Guy Fawkes, who aimed to blow up Parliament. While many Londoners would agree over a pint of ale that this might have been a good idea, every Fifth of November, Guy Fawkes Day, celebrates the fact that the Londoner feels it is something which is "not done". Police regulations have it that no major demonstration can approach the Houses of Parliament. The Londoner agrees, and should any pressure group from outside attempt to break the rule, its members are dispersed by police who do not even draw their truncheons, secure that they have the citizenry on their side.

This calm of the Londoner, his refusal to join in the sweat and the shouting, often strikes foreigners as strange. And well it might. When I first visited Washington D.C., I was warned by my New York friends that I would be bored to death because I would hear nothing but politics. They were quite right. On the other hand, my first visit to New York coincided with the election of a Governor of New York State. People talked of nothing else. I was not bored: New York's acid wit about its politicians is a joy to hear. You will not find the same in London, should you be there during a General Election. I have seen a million people turn out to greet a Prime Minister in New Delhi. Such a multitude has only once assembled in London for a British Prime Minister. That was for Winston Churchill, and then, be it noted, for his funeral.

I know that I should explain, in clear and simple words, what makes the Londoner tick—tick, that is, with the even, unalterable rhythm of the huge clock on the tower of his Houses of Parliament. I shall not be able to do it, because nobody can; the Londoner himself never tries. But perhaps a simile will help. When that great clock was first put up, more than a century ago, it did not run true. Then somebody put a single halfpenny on the weights; and all was well. From then until now it has kept perfect time. It seems to me that, in much the same way, the Londoner has added some

Knee deep in the thick grass of Richmond Park, a red deer of the Queen's herd imperiously surveys its domain, ignoring the tower blocks of suburban Roehampton. There are fallow deer as well as the red deer in Richmond Park, which at 2,400 acres is the largest of the Royal Parks.

special touch of his own to western urban man, a touch that gives him balance. One side of the coin is no doubt his sense of humour, the other his knowledge that he has led the civilized world, and that his place in history is secure.

I would like to show you one last great monument of which the Londoner is justly proud. It is Westminster Abbey, and one of his favourites.

Inside, it is a fine piece of Gothic, and if the outside is largely the work of 19th and 20th Century restorers, it has been creditably done. Still, architecture does not concern the Londoner much. It never has, and more's the pity. But the Abbey is a very human church. It is the place of royal weddings and funerals, which the Londoner remembers. It is the place, too, of coronations. In the past, the ordinary citizen saw nothing of this ceremony. Nowadays he can see the whole thing sitting at home watching television, and much better than those present who can see only bits of it. But much nearer to the Londoner than all the pomp is a manuscript book that is kept there. It contains the names of those who died in the bombings. A page is turned every day, and he might well see the name of someone he knew or loved as a child. It warms the place for him.

There is humour and quirkishness in the Abbey, too—both beloved of the Londoner. The place is full of monuments of the great, and those who supposed themselves great. They have little appeal. Often it seems that the bigger the rogue the bigger his monument. But there are others. Each will have his favourites. Here are mine, and James Hanaway heads my list. He died, his monument tells us, in 1786. He lies among the great solely because he was a London original. He was the first man to dare to carry an umbrella in the streets of London. He got into trouble, especially from coachmen and sedan chairmen who correctly foresaw a threat to their livelihood. But he persisted. The umbrella became the symbol of the Londoner and stayed so until these recent decades. The Londoner even took it abroad with him and waved it at foreigners to get that service which he considered his due. I also like the slab that marks the grave of George Peabody, the only American to be buried in the Abbey. He is not there now; his body was carried off to Massachusetts in a British man-'o-war. He deserved his honours. He shamed London over its slums. He built, out of his own pocket, blocks of flats for some, at least, of the poor to live in.

Clive of India is buried here. But so also is John Herschel. His father discovered a new planet, but *his* son discovered that you can catch criminals by their fingerprints—something more useful than Uranus and more permanent than the work of Clive. Out in the cloisters is another grave, that of John Broughton. He was a famous pugilist in the 18th Century. He must have been a fine figure of a man, because a sculptor used him as a model for Hercules. Sport-loving Londoners had him buried among the great. They wanted to put "Champion of England" on his tombstone but the Dean grew stuffy, and the proud epitaph was never carved. Here, too, is the effigy of Queen Elizabeth I, a copy of that carried in her funeral procession. Perhaps it was done by an incompetent sculptor; on the other hand, I find it intriguing to reflect that she might very well have been as ugly as that.

There is, of course, the throne of England, and he or she who sits on it makes history. Somebody else once made history in the Abbey, too. He sat on the Archbishop of Canterbury. He did this in the chapel of St. Catherine, of which today there are only a few arches left and a door in the Little Cloister. It once closed on a piquant scene. The incident took place in the reign of Henry II. The King was hearing mass in the Abbey proper. The Archbishops of York and Canterbury were in the chapel. The Archbishop of York thought himself equal to the Archbishop of Canterbury. When he saw Canterbury take his seat before him, he was enraged. He firmly planted himself on Canterbury's lap and refused to move. He was dragged off and hit by a bystander, whereupon he rushed into the Abbey, accosted the praying King and complained. Henry took the matter with a good-natured laugh. He agreed that the Archbishop of York should be called the Primate of England, which satisfied him. But the king also said that Canterbury should be called the Primate of *All* England. And down to this day, these two eminent ecclesiastics are so called.

Of all the stories that can be told about London, that is the one I like most. An odd choice, perhaps, but then I was brought up in this great city: I cannot help having an irreverent sense of humour.

Now I must add an epilogue. Although I lived for 28 years of my life in London, I left its cloudy skies and went to live in Italy. But I have come back again and again, sometimes to stay for months on end. Each time, before I leave London, I like to take a walk, a long London walk, such as can be taken in no other city of the world. I take a walk in the country, but I stay, all the time, in the very heart of London.

I start at Westminster. I put the Parliament and the Abbey behind me and in a minute or two I am in St. James's Park. Everybody knows that the Prime Minister lives at No. 10 Downing Street. This park is his back garden. He has a small one of his own, but only a wall divides it from St. James's Park. You can study some of nature's more eccentric creations there: penguins, pelicans and politicians. These latter can often be seen strolling, two by two, after a Cabinet session in near-by No. 10.

The park itself was designed by John Nash, and it is one of his creations that neither bombs nor developers can destroy. It is superbly English. The Boboli Garden in Florence is really a sculpture gallery for pieces too big for the Pitti Palace. The gardens of Versailles are designed to show how even nature obeyed the Sun King. The Shalimar in Kashmir is very beautiful, but one is conscious all the time that its object was to give the Great Mogul a bit of cool at midday. John Nash left nature alone as much as he possibly could. As with those other two English masters of landscape planning, William Beckford and Capability Brown, you feel that they almost apologize for cutting a path. St. James's echoes the softness of Kent and Hampshire and Sussex.

There is a long lake running through it, with a bridge. I take my last look at London from the middle of this bridge. The cupolas of the Italian palaces of Whitehall blend, it seems by accident, into a view that takes one back to the Mediterranean. Siena in an autumn mist is one of the world's loveliest sights. Here, in the same season, London can be its equal.

I walk the length of the park. I cross briefly in front of Buckingham Palace with its sentries, but I am in no mood for the trappings of royalty. I am immediately among grass fields again. This second open space has not been designed; it preserves, right beside Piccadilly, the air of a village green. Indeed, it is called Green Park.

At the very end of Green Park London bursts upon me with a roar. There are streets to cross, but full in view, beckoning me on, is a portico of classic elegance, with the figures on the frieze calm and inviting above the traffic. Sixty seconds and I am through this gateway and in Hyde Park.

I am in the country again, a great swathe of it, four miles round. Here, as I climb slopes and go down them, I have the immemorial contours of London under my feet. It is a city built on low hills, smothered now, except here. I pass under the shadows of great trees. I see water, and the coloured sails of boats. I cross another bridge, the most graceful in London, and I am still in the country. The park changes a little, as it changes its name. Here, in Kensington Gardens, there are more studied perspectives, but paths still wander across meadows. I come to a pond with children sailing boats, in the same place that England's most inspired child, Shelley, folded banknotes to make his own boats and set them sailing.

I am near the end of my walk. I am tired, but there, ahead of me, is a pavilion. It is called the Orangery, and inside there are orange trees. It was built in the 18th Century; it is white, refreshing and perfect. Roman statues stand in niches. A great Roman urn stands in the middle. Like the men who made this beautiful place, my thoughts go southwards to the sun, to the Latin lands.

It is time to go, as I have gone many times before. But how eagerly I shall accept an invitation to return.

The Candid London

Feathers grace the head of Eros in Piccadilly Circus (left), as well as the dress hat of the Tower of London's Governor, who suggests some exotic bird.

A city and its people reveal themselves in the most telling—and entertaining—fashion when caught off guard. Sometimes London's stolid statues can be as intriguing as the human tide that moves around them, when seen in the sidelong glance of a candid photograph. To walk through the city with open eyes, alert to the haphazard sights and random combinations of past and present, is to see London in a revealing light. The spontaneous gestures of young and old, and even the frozen attitudes of imposing memorials, can present the city in a fresh and delightfully unexpected light. As the photographs on these pages prove, the camera enhances this illusion by freezing the moment of movement, thereby demonstrating that London can by turns be grotesque and touching, comic and elegiac—and, most of all, a city with a character unlike any other in the world.

Perpetually adorning the dim pavements of Parliament Square, Jan Christiaan Smuts and Winston Churchill (background) are visited at sunrise by a duck.

On a suburban lawn a bowls player lists at an angle, urging on his ball by the power of concentrated thought.

By a flower-garlanded pergola in Regent's Park stands a glossy bronze conceit: a helmeted cherub preparing to dispatch a vulture struggling under his weight.

By the tiled wall of a Victorian pub in a littered side-street a modern child of the city in jacket and jeans finds an innocent target for his aggressive fantasy.

Even strong men defer to the commanding gesture of a "lollipop lady", striding imperiously across her rightful territory, her STOP sign gripped like a standard.

Impelled by his missionary zeal, a solitary man expounds his convictions at Speakers' Corner, undeterred by the inattention of his audience of one.

During a concert interval at the Royal Albert Hall two lovers embrace, oblivious of the window framing them.

A house of London brick, empty while it awaits renovation, has been given a temporary life in colour by an unknown artist parodying the city's domesticity.

Bibliography

Banks, F. R., *The Penguin Guide to London.* Penguin Books, 1971.

Barker, Felix and Jackson, Peter, *London—2000 Years of a City and Its People.* Cassell & Co., London, 1974.

Betjeman, John, *Victorian and Edwardian London.* B. T. Batsford, London, 1969.

Brown, Ivor, *London.* Newnes, London, 1960.

Corporation of London, *London Bridge.* 1967.

Dodson, M., and Saczek, R., *A Dictionary of Cockney Slang and Rhyming Slang.* Hedgehog Enterprises, London, 1972.

Dyos, H. J., and Wolff, Michael, *The Victorian City: Images and Realities (2 vols.).* Routledge & Kegan Paul, London, 1974.

Evelyn, John, *The Diary of John Evelyn.* ed. William Bray, Everyman's Library, J. M. Dent & Sons, London, 1973.

Fletcher, Bannister, *A History of Architecture on the Comparative Method.* The Athlone Press, London, 1961.

Gaunt, William, *London.* B. T. Batsford, London, 1961.

Henrey, Mrs. Robert, *London Under Fire 1940-45.* J. M. Dent & Sons, London, 1969.

Hibbert, Christopher, *London—The Biography of a City.* Longman, London, 1969.

Kent, William, *An Encyclopaedia of London.* J. M. Dent & Sons, London, 1970.

Margetson, Stella, *Regency London.* Cassell & Co., London, 1974.

Mitchell, R. J., and Leys, M. D. R., *A History of London Life.* Penguin Books, 1964.

Morton, H. V., *In Search of London.* Methuen & Co., London, 1951.

Nicholson's Guide to the Thames. Robert Nicholson Publications.

Pepys, Samuel, *The Diary of Samuel Pepys (3 vols.).* ed. John Warrington, Everyman's Library, J. M. Dent & Sons, London, 1971.

Pevsner, Nikolaus, *The Buildings of England, London (Vol. 1).* Revised Edition Bridget Cherry, Penguin Books, 1975.

Pevsner, Nikolaus, *The Buildings of England, London (Vol. II).* Penguin Books, 1952.

Piper, David, *London.* Thames and Hudson, London, 1971.

Piper, David, *The Companion Guide to London.* Fontana, London, 1972.

Rose, Millicent, *The East End of London.* New Portway Reprints, 1973.

Rossiter, Stuart, *The Blue Guide to London.* Ernest Benn, 1973.

Rude, George, *Hanoverian London, 1714-1808.* Secker & Warburg, London, 1971.

Simms, Eric, *Wildlife in the Royal Parks.* H.M.S.O., 1974.

Smith, Raymond, *The Living City—A New View of the City of London.* Corporation of London, 1957.

Summerson, John, *Georgian London.* Barrie & Jenkins, London, 1970.

Wesker, Arnold and Allin, John, *Say Goodbye You May Never See Them Again.* Jonathan Cape, London, 1974.

Whinney, Margaret, *Wren.* Thames and Hudson, London, 1971.

Williams, George, *Guide to Literary London.* B. T. Batsford, London, 1973.

Willmott, Peter and Young, Michael, *Family and Class in a London Suburb.* Routledge & Kegan Paul, London, 1960.

Acknowledgements and Picture Credits

The editors wish to thank the following: Baltic Exchange, London; Debbie Beaver, Bethnal Green Museum, London; Michael Bodenham, Floris Ltd., London; Corporation of the City of London; Charles Dettmer, Thames Ditton, Surrey; Geoffrey Ennals, Port of London Authority; Department of the Environment, London; Jim Hicks, London; Household Division, Brigade of Guards, London; Leighton House Museum, London; Lloyds of London; James Lock & Co., London; Doris Mason, Shenfield, Essex; Alan Mehegan, Port of London Authority; Houses of Parliament Library, London.

Sources for pictures in this book are shown below. Credits for the pictures from left to right are separated by commas; from top to bottom they are separated by dashes.

All the photographs are by Brian Seed except: Cover—Jay Maisel. Page 7—by kind permission of the British Library Board. 8—(bottom) Daily Telegraph Colour Library. London. 10, 11—Anthony Edgeworth—Roy Williams (insert). 12—by kind permission of the British Library Board. 14, 15—map by Anna Pugh. 16—Larry Burrows from Aspect Picture Library Ltd., London. 26, 27—Daily Telegraph Colour Library, London. 29—Adam Woolfitt from Susan Griggs Picture Agency, London. 30, 31—Robert Estall. 33—Roy Williams. 34—George Rodger from Magnum Photos. 39—Imperial War Museum, London-Fox Photos, London. 40—Patrick Thurston. 42, 43—*Old England. A Museum of Popular Antiquities.* Vol. II edited by Charles Knight. 48—Patrick Ward. 49—Laurie Lewis. 51—Patrick Ward. 52—Adam Woolfitt from Susan Griggs Picture Agency, London. 54—Laurie Lewis. 63—Derek Bayes, courtesy of Bethnal Green Museum, London. 65—Derek Bayes. 66, 67—Laurie Lewis. 70 to 77—Mary Evans Picture Library, London. 81—Patrick Ward. 82, 83—(top) pics. 1, 3, 5, Lou Klein—(middle) all Lou Klein—(bottom) pics. 2, 3, 4, Lou Klein. 85—Patrick Thurston. 86—Anthony Edgeworth. 88—(top) Luis Villota. 101—Lou Klein. 102—Patrick Thurston. 104—Patrick Thurston. 107 to 109—Anthony Blake. 111—Adam Woolfitt from Susan Griggs Picture Agency, London. 113—Anthony Blake. 116 to 118—John Garrett. 121, 122—Patrick Ward. 124, 125—John Garrett. 126—Daily Telegraph Colour Library, London. 128—by kind permission of the Savoy Hotel Ltd., London. 136—Patrick Ward. 139—Laurie Lewis. 140—Holmer W. Sykes. 143—Radio Times Hulton Picture Library, London. 146 to 155—Laurie Lewis. 158—Mary Evans Picture Library, London. 162, 163—Patrick Thurston. 168 to 176—Patrick Thurston. 178—Mary Evans Picture Library, London. 179—Daily Telegraph Colour Library, London. 180—Dale Brown. 183, 184—Patrick Thurston. 193—Laurie Lewis. 195—Patrick Ward. 197—Jasmine Spencer. Last end paper—Anthony Edgeworth.

Index

Numerals in italics indicate a photograph or drawing of the subject mentioned.

A
Adam, Robert, 44, 45
Adelphi, the, 45
Albert Memorial, *160-1*, 164
Albert, Prince Consort, 87, 89, 164
Architecture: Baroque, 41-2; in the City, 17, 21; Classical, 164, 165; English Perpendicular, 161; "Georgian", 57, 58, 60, 66; Gothic, 21, 36, 41, 161, 164, 165, 185; "Neo-Georgian", 68; Palladian, 44-5; Victorian, 66-8, 161-5
Art galleries, 113-14
Athenaeum, *126-7*, 128, 130

B
Bank of England, 19
Barry, Sir Charles, 164, 165
Battersea Power Station, *30-1*
Bedford Square, 58-60
Beefeaters, 8, *82-3*
Betjeman, John, 69
Big Ben, *4-5*, *8-9*, 165, 184
Billingsgate, 9, 21, *72-3*
Bloomsbury, 35, 58-60, 112
Boadicea, 6, 8
Bond Street, 103, *106-7*, 113
Boodle's, 128
Bow Bells, 21, 138
Bowler hats and umbrellas, 13, *78-9*, *113*, 134
British Empire, 13, 68-9, 158, 167
Brooks's, 127
Bryanston Square, *182-3*
Buckingham Palace, *10-11*, 36, 60, 89, 90, 93, *101*, 137, 161, 187
Bull and Bush, 142
Burlington Arcade, *106-7*, 110
Buskers, *146-7*, *147*, *148-55*

C
Campden Hill, 66
Carnaby Street, 5, 138, 142
Cenotaph, the, *159*, 166
Changing of the Guard, *10-11*
Chaplin, Charlie, 140, 142
Charing Cross, 6, 157
Charles I, 17, 157, 184
Charles II, 9, *12-13*, 17, 37-8, 40, 41, 89
Cheapside, 21, 79
Chelsea Flower Show, *66-7*
Chelsea Pensioners, 50, *88*
Chelsea Royal Hospital, *67*
Churches: Great St. Helen's, 9-13, 16; St. Bartholomew's, 37; St. Botolph's, *34-5*; St. Bride's, *42-3*; St. James's, *cover*; St. Mary-le-Bow, 21, *42-3*; Southwark Cathedral, 139; *see also* St. Paul's Cathedral; Westminster Abbey
Churchill, Sir Winston, 161, 166, 179-81, 184, *190*
City, the, 6-9, 79; architecture, 17, 21; growth of, 16; merchants, 12-13, 16, 18-20; offices, 19, *19-20*; relationship to the Government, 18; worldwide faith in, 20
Club Row, *153*

Clubs, *126-7*, 137; disestablishmentarianism on, 132-5; membership selection and regulations, 128-9; origin of, 127-8; preparation for, 129-32; purpose of, 128-9
Cobbett, William, 61
Cockneys, *54*, *75*, *136-7*, *139*, *140*; culture of, 140, 141, 144-5; definition of, 21; dialect of, 138, 139, 140-1, 144, 145; entertainment, 141-4; humour of, 141-2; origin of name, 138; in Victorian times, 138-9
College of Arms, 79-80, 84, 86, 89
Commons, House of, 86, 165, 177, *179*
Constitution, British, 182
Coronations, 91
County Hall, *172*, *173*
Covent Garden, 103, 128
Cricket, *130-1*
Cromwell, Oliver, 37
Crystal Palace, 35-6

D
Dark House Lane, *72-3*
Dickens, Charles, 58, 61, 76, 127, 139
Dockland, *26-7*, *28*, *29*, *39*
Doré, Gustav, 71
Downing Street, *176-7*, 186
Duke of Edinburgh, 89

E
Ealing, *56-7*
Earl Marshal, 84, 91
East End, 61, 62, 152; *see also* Cockneys; Dockland
Edward VII, 86, 87
Edward VIII, 87
Elizabeth I, 12, 57, 91, 185-6
Elizabeth II, 13, 36, 86-7, 88, 89
Eros, *102-3*, *104*, 105, 188
Establishment, the, 127, 132-3, 134, 135
Evelyn, John, 37, 38, 40, 61

F
Fashion, 134-5
Fawkes, Guy, 178, 184
Fire of London, *see* Great Fire of London
Foot Guards, 79, *84-5*, *88*
Foreign Office, 165
Fox, Charles James, 127-8
Friday Street, 21

G
George V, 6, 87-8, 91
George VI, 137
Gilbert, Sir Alfred, 104
Gladstone, William, 64, 66, 179
Gordon Riots, 184
Gray's Inn, 58
Great Exhibition of 1851, 35, 164
Great Fire of London, 9, 15, 35, 36; efforts to contain, 38; extent of destruction, 38-40, 45; origins of, 37
Great Plague of London, 37
Green Park, 187
Gresham, Sir Thomas, 12
Grosvenor Square, 60
Guard officers, *11*, 13, *55*; tunics of, 87; *see*

also Foot Guards; Queen's Household Cavalry
Guildhall, 21, 166
Guilds, *see* Livery Companies
Guy Fawkes Day, 184
Gwyn, Nell, 9, 36

H
Hampstead Heath, 45, 142
Hampton Court, *32*
Haymarket Theatre, *104*
Heralds, *see* College of Arms
Heren, Louis, 61-2
Holland House, *39*, 66
Holland Park, 66-7
Horse Guards Parade, *78-9*, *84-5*, *176-7*
Household Cavalry, *see* Queen's Household Cavalry
Houses of Parliament, 24, 84, 86, 164-5, *172*, 177, *179*
Hyde Park, 5, 35, 44, 93, *116-17*, 117, *121-5*, 158, *171*, 187

I
Immigrants, 167
Imperial Standards of Length, 158
Imperial State Crown, 6, 86, *156-7*
Inns of Court, 36, 57-8

J
James I, 87, 178
Jellied eels, *49*
Jerrold, Blanchard, 71
Johnson, Dr. Samuel, 129, 157, 184
Judd, Sir Andrew, 12

K
Kensington, *64-5*, 66
Kensington Gardens, 44-5, *120*, 187
Kenwood House, 45
Kirwin, William, 13

L
Lambeth, 142
Landseer, Sir Edwin, 158
Leighton, Frederick, 67, 68, 69
Leighton House, 67-8
Life Guards, *99*
Lincoln's Inn, 58
Livery Companies, 17-18
Lloyd George, David, 89, 181
Lloyd's of London, 20-1
Lombard Street, 17
London: decline of status, 166-7; Elizabethan, 36-7; "Golden Age" of, 159; growth of, 6, 57; history of, 6, 8, 36-7; maps of, *14*, *15*; population of, 6; rebuilding of, after Great Fire, 40-2, 44-5, 57; residential districts of, *58-9*, *143* (*see also* Slums; Suburbs); size of, 5-6; "Swinging", 5, 135; Victorian, 61-8, *70-7*, 143
London Bridge, old, *6-7*, 139
Londoners: 21, *46-7*, 47, *48-55*, 61, 71, 74, 75, *133*, *191*, *193-6*; attitudes of, towards London, 5, 6, 36, 159; attitudes of, towards monarchy, 87-91; calmness of, 35, 36, 40, 45; change in character of, 138; pride of, 177, 182, 184-5; reserve of, 182, 184; in World War II,

166-7; *see also* City merchants; Cockneys; Shopkeepers; Theatregoers
Lord Mayor of London, 12, 16-17, 18, 20, 21, 37, 67
Lord Mayor's Banquet, 18, 20
Lord's cricket ground, 8
Lords, House of, 86

M
MacDonald, Ramsay, 91, 177
Mall, the, *55, 84-5, 99,* 137
Mansion House, 21
Mayfair, 57, *58,* 105
Memorial, Albert, *160-1,* 164
Milk Street, 21
Monarchy, 87-91; *see also* Elizabeth II
Monument, the, 9, *12-13,* 17, 37, 45
Monuments, 157-61, *168-75;* in Westminster Abbey, 185-6; *see also* Architecture; Statues
More, Sir Thomas, 21
Museums, *164,* 167
Music halls, 142, 147

N
Nash, John, 44-5, 137, 186
Nelson's Column, 157, 158, *158-9,* 161, *170*
Newton, Isaac, 41

O
Old Kent Road, 140
Opening of Parliament, 84-7

P
Pageantry, *front end-paper,* 80, 84, *84-5,* 86-7, 91; *see also* Queen's Household Cavalry
Painting, Victorian, 67, 69
Palaces: Buckingham Palace, *10-11,* 36, 90; in the City, 16; Palace of St. James, 137; Palace of Westminster, *see* Houses of Parliament
Pall Mall, 127, 132, 135, 164
Park Lane, 104
Parks, *15,* 44-5; Green Park, 187; Hampstead Heath, 45, 142; Hyde Park, 5, 35, 44, 93, *116-17,* 117, *121-5,* 158, *171,* 187; Kensington Gardens, 44-5, *120,* 187; Regent's Park, 44-5, 117, *119,* 192; Richmond Park, *184;* St. James's Park, *118, 156-7, 176-7,* 186-7
Parliament and parliamentary procedure, 6, 18, 84-7, 177-82
Paternoster Row, 38
Pavement artists, *154,* 155
Paxton, Sir Joseph, 35
Pearly King and Queen, *136-7,* 140, 142
Petticoat Lane, *152*
Philip, Duke of Edinburgh, 89

Piccadilly Circus, *102-3,* 104, 130, 188
Port of London, 23
Portman Square, 60
Portobello Road, *149*
Pubs, *62, 133,* 138, 142, 145, *193, back endpaper*
Pugin, Augustus, 164, 165

Q
Quant, Mary, 134-5
Queen Anne's Gate, 58
Queen's Household Cavalry, *81, 92-3, 93, 94-101*
Queen's Speech, 86

R
Regent Street, 44
Regent's Park, 44-5, 117, *119,* 192
Restaurants, 115, *128,* 130
Rhyming slang, 141, 144
Richmond Park, *184*
Rotherhithe, *26-7*
Rowlands, Samuel, 138
Royal Albert Hall, *162-3, 196*
Royal Coat of Arms, *82-3,* 84
Royal Courts of Justice, 165
Royal Exchange, 12
Royal Family, 81, 87-91
Royal Horticultural Society, *66-7*
Royal Peculiar, the, 174
Royal Society, 38, 40, 41
Royal Society of Arts, 45
Russell Square, 60

S
St. Bartholomew's Church, 37
St. Botolph's Church, *34-5*
St. Bride's Church, *42-3*
St. James's Palace, 137
St. James's Church, *cover*
St. James's Park, *118, 156-7,* 186-7
St. Mary-le-Bow Church, 21, *42-3,* 138
St. Pancras Railway Station, 165
St. Paul's Cathedral, 36, 161, *174;* destruction of, by Great Fire, 37, 38, 40; rebuilding of, after Great Fire, 41-2, *42-3,* 44
Savage Club, 128
Scott, Sir George Gilbert, 165
Scott, Sir Giles Gilbert, 30
Serpentine, the, *116-17, 122, 124*
Shaftesbury Avenue, 105, 108, 114
Shaftesbury, Lord, 104, 105
Shaw, George Bernard, 108, 140, 144
Shops and shopkeepers, *108-9, 110-11,* 110-13
Simpson's in the Strand, *128,* 130
Slums: pre-war, 61-2; Victorian, *71,* 143
Smithfield Market, *54*
Soho, 105, 114-15

Southwark Cathedral, 139
Speaker's Corner, 158, *195*
Staper, Richard, 12
Staple Inn, 36-7
Statues, 189, *189,* 192; Charles I, 157; Charles II, 12-13; Churchill, Winston, 161, *190;* Eros, *102-3,* 104, 105, *188-9;* "Fat Boy", 45; Smuts, Jan Christiaan, *190*
Strand, the, 57, 58, 130
Street entertainers, *see* Buskers
Street-traders, Victorian, *74, 75*
Suburbs, 62-4; inner, *56-7,* 64-6; outer, 20, 32, 66-7, 68-9
Syon House, *33*

T
Temple, the, 58
Temple Bar, 16
Thames, River, 4-7, 15, 23, *22-23*
Theatre and theatregoers, 103, *104,* 105-10, 141
Threadneedle Street, 9, 12, 17
Throne of England, 186
Tower Bridge, 24, *25,* 33, 169, *169*
Tower of London, 6-7, 16, *40, 168,* 169
Trafalgar Square, 137, 138, 157-8, *158, 159,* 164, *170*
Treasury, the, 18
Trooping the Colour, *front endpaper, 84-5*

U
University College, London, 35

V
Victoria, Queen, 16, 35, 61, 71, 87, 164; Jubilee, 66, 87
Victoria and Albert Museum, *164,* 167
Vincent Square, *130-1*

W
Wapping, 62
West End, 61-2, 103, *103,* 104-5, 127; *see also* Restaurants; Shops and shopkeepers; Soho; Theatre and theatregoers
Westminster, 16, 57, 58
Westminster Abbey, 87, 91, 161, *174-5,* 185-6
Westminster Bridge, *22-3*
Westminster, Palace of, *see* Houses of Parliament
Whitechapel, 5, 61, 140
Whitehall, *4-5,* 16, *99, 101,* 157, *159,* 161, 165, 184
White's, 127
Whittington, Dick, 16, 21
Windsor, Duke and Duchess of, 87
Windsor, House of, 89
Woburn Walk, 112
Wren, Sir Christopher, 40-2, 44, 45, 80

Colour reproduction by Printing Developments International Ltd., Leeds, England—a Time Inc. subsidiary.
Filmsetting by C. E. Dawkins (Typesetters) Ltd., London, SE1 1UN.
Printed and bound in Italy (March 1976) by Arnoldo Mondadori, Verona.   I